# Vedanta
# Examples
# Simplified

SUKHDEV VIRDEE

# DEDICATION

Dedicated to the Absolute Divine
Truth That **YOU** Are!

Whole heartedly dedicated to
Lord Krishna, Lord Shiva,
Sri Ramana Maharshi and
Guru Nanak Dev Ji who have been and are
My Spiritual Guides on the path to
Self Realization and God Realization.

# CONTENTS

# ACKNOWLEDGMENTS

There are three friends that I have to absolutely acknowledge who knowingly or unknowingly led me to realize the Absolute Truth.

The first is Vik Sharma, the most hyperactive friend I have. He introduced me to Lord Krishna.

The second friend is Rajeev Aryan, an awakened being himself. He introduced me to the Bhagavad Gita and predicted that I would soon have a similar awakening.
This led to Self-Realization through complete surrender, love and devotion.

The third friend is Ranjan Sahu, a living encyclopedia of Spiritual Scriptures. He was sent by Lord Krishna to guide me on the path of knowledge, the Highest Truth.
This led to God-Realization through direct experiential knowledge.

# INTRODUCTION

Advaita Vedanta Examples are a great way to illustrate what the Absolute Reality called Brahman can be *'like'*. However if the examples are not presented clearly, they can and often lead to misunderstandings, which further leads to deeper confusion for the genuine seeker.

The examples can become very confusing because there is nothing to *'directly'* relate to, even after listening to the examples. The examples use *objects* that we know and can relate to from *our* point of view as a person, but Brahman cannot be known or perceived in any way.

Furthermore, if the examples aren't explained in a clear manner, it will leave the listener or reader with a lot more questions than before. As they try to understand one point another three questions arise and one gets entangled.

It is important to realize that every example that is presented will be understood by your mind and intellect but when it comes to Brahman, your mind and intellect cannot understand it. Many seekers get stuck trying to 'understand' Brahman just as they understand the examples, by tying to use their mind and intellect.

The examples have to be understood by the mind but Brahman has to be *realized* not understood. To understand anything you need to use your mind and intellect, but realization is the act of becoming fully aware of something *as a fact*.

It is almost like the difference between knowledge and wisdom. Knowledge is, knowing that a tomato is a fruit, and wisdom is, knowing not to put it in a fruit salad.

As you go through the examples you may realize that certain words have been repeated again and again. This is done purposely to leave no room for doubt or a question to creep in. For example, seekers of the truth hear this all the time, *"You are the absolute truth but you just don't know it."*

Such a statement can be very confusing for someone who doesn't know what he or she *doesn't know.* A clearer way of putting the same statement would be, *"You (as Brahman) are the absolute truth but you (as the person) just don't know it."*

The examples included in this book are some of the most common ones used in Vedanta. Although there are many more apart from the ones presented here, if you understand these, it is unlikely that you will have any difficulty understanding any other. In fact you would be on your way to making up your own examples.

One more thing that should be kept in mind, if you are a seeking the truth of who you are or what this Universe and God are, make sure to keep your mind focused on attaining that specific goal and not getting into arguments about what could have, would have or should have been in these examples.

Ponder over the examples in your daily activities and try to understand them better using what's in front of you at the time. For example, instead of clay and pot, you may be used to seeing more plastic objects around you. Replace clay with plastic, and pot with bottle, and see if it works, and you'll find that it does!

Finally, the examples have been presented in a story format so that your power of visualization and imagination are fully engaged as you read the book. Visuals flashing through your mind while the mental voice reads the book will enhance your reading and understanding.

Happy reading.......

# Vedanta Examples Simplified

Vedanta Examples Simplified

# ASANTE SANA

*"And for the next performance we have the very popular rock band all the way from California. Please put your hands together for Asante Sana!"* announced the emcee on stage. Four band members walked up as a crowd of over twenty thousand young college boys and girls cheered and applauded.

Several Universities and Colleges from all over the world took part in the prestigious *International Rock Festival* and this year it was being hosted in the Indian state of Goa, also popularly known as *'Pearl of the Orient'* or a *'Tourist Paradise'.*

The wonderful beaches and hotels on the coastline, the nightlong parties, the great weather and very hospitable local people make Goa a very popular tourist destination.

The cheer grew louder as an American boy *(Nelson)*, an African boy *(Asher)*, an Indian boy *(Suraj)* and a young elegant looking Brazilian girl *(Eloa)* walked on to the stage. *Asante Sana* was a popular rock band that already enjoyed a huge fan following on all the social media platforms.

Thousands of fans appreciated the multi-racial band for their high-energy live performances but more importantly they loved the fact that the band members got along with each other despite coming from different countries and backgrounds. The crowd went crazy as *Asante Sana* took to the stage and started their performance with their most popular hit song.

Nelson was a local boy from California who loved playing the drums. Asher was the main lead vocalist hailing from Kenya who always dreamt of being the lead singer in a band. He helped put this band together and also gave it its name. *Asante Sana* is a popular Swahili phrase meaning, *'Thank You Very Much'*.

Suraj was from *Rishikesh* in India. He was in the University of California to complete his Masters in Commerce. Eloa was from Brazil. She was tall and beautiful with the voice of an angel. Asher had noticed her at one of the college functions where she sang the national anthem and approached her to join the band.

Nelson fell in love with Eloa the moment he met her at their first rehearsal. They started dating soon after. Suraj was the geek in the band. He wore big black glasses and had buckteeth. He had a great sense of humor and was the funny guy in the band. *Asante Sana* was a perfect blend of talent, glamour, good looks and fun.

College girls drooled over Nelson's deep blue eyes, tall and slender body with a handsome face. He was lovable and sweet, and he played the drums with great passion. The male fans were crazy about Eloa. She always dressed up very elegantly and carried herself with great poise. With long brown flowing hair, high boots and a sweet smile, she looked really adorable while playing the bass guitar as she sang.

Asher, the main singer had a deep husky voice that touched one's soul instantly. He was tall and played the lead guitar as he sang. Suraj always hid himself behind the keyboards and enjoyed interacting with the other band members on stage, trying to keep his mind off the audience.

*"And for our last performance tonight we'll be singing our latest single, 'Let's talk about love', that is currently trending in the top ten most popular songs on social media thanks to you guys. If you know the lyrics please sing along with us,"* announced Asher. The lyrics were displayed on the giant screen behind them and a chorus of twenty thousand people sang the entire song with them.

*"Wow!"* Exclaimed Nelson as they walked off the stage. *"That last song gave me goose bumps. Do you believe twenty thousand people just sang our song together? I'm still in shock!"* *"This is the biggest audience we have ever performed for, it was always going to be spectacular,"* said Eloa as they got into their car and were driven to their hotel.

They were on holiday for two weeks and had planned to tour a few places in India during their stay. They spent the next two days going to the festival to watch the other rock bands that were performing. They partied in Goa for another two nights and experienced the all night parties that went on at secret venues and others that took place on the open beaches.

*"I have to go and visit my parents in Rishikesh. They know I'm here and I haven't seen them in two years,"* said Suraj to the rest of them. *"You guys can carry on with the tour as planned but I'm sorry I can't go back without meeting my parents,"* said Suraj, his eyes getting moist.

*"I thought you were going to be with us throughout the trip,"* said Nelson putting his arm around Eloa as they sipped fresh coconut water on the beach under the blazing sun. *"Sounds like you're dumping us in your own country,"* said Asher in his Kenyan accent.

*"I know,"* said Suraj, *"I'm sorry but my heart says I have to go and see them. I'm not dumping you. You can carry on with the trip as planned and I can always be in touch on the phone. But if you like you can join me. My parents live alone; we have a huge bungalow with extra rooms in Rishikesh that can accommodate all of us. After staying a few days with them we can visit the other places before returning to Goa in time for our flight,"* said Suraj.

*"Are you sure?"* asked Asher, *"Your family won't mind us staying at your house?"* *"Not at all,"* replied Suraj immediately, *"In fact they will be happy to meet you all. I'll even organize the tickets to and from Rishikesh,"* said Suraj.

*"Is it a tourist destination? Is there anything worthwhile seeing there? I don't want to get bored sitting at your home doing nothing,"* said Eloa.

*"Oh! Rishikesh is a very popular tourist destination but not in the way that Goa is. Rishikesh is known as the 'Yoga and meditation capital of the world'. It's a spiritual and sacred pilgrimage place. So there won't be any all night parties, alcohol or any non-vegetarian food,"* said Suraj with a smile on his face.

*"I'm not really bothered about booze and partying. I love yoga and would love to see how it's done in India. But I'll come only if you have a separate room for Nelson and me. I won't share a room with anyone else,"* said Eloa looking at Nelson who held her hand and gave it a kiss.

*"That's great,"* replied Suraj, *"Like I said, we have extra rooms. You can have the single room on the terrace. It has a great view of the Ganges River and the lights of the city at night,"* said Suraj. *"What do you say Asher?"* asked Nelson, *"Well I guess it should be fine. We can always leave if we get bored. I love visiting spiritual places and since Suraj is footing the bill, count me in,"* said Asher.

*"That's great! I'll book our tickets for tomorrow morning. We'll take the morning flight to Delhi and then hire a taxi to Rishikesh. We'll be there by tomorrow evening. I'll just call my parents and inform them. They will be so happy. Thank you guys. Asante sana!"* Exclaimed an excited Suraj, as he quickly got busy on his phone.

*"Namaste Dad. I'm in Goa. Yes, the show was great. Yes, I'm fine. Listen, we're all coming to Rishikesh tomorrow. Yes, the four of us. We'll stay a few days with you and then carry on with the rest of the tour. Can I ask Ishaan uncle to book our tickets and the cab from Delhi please? Thank you Dad, you're the best. I'll call when we leave from Delhi. See you tomorrow Dad. Love you too,"* said Suraj as he disconnected the phone and quickly called Ishaan uncle who was their regular travel agent to give him the details. Within an hour all their travel bookings were messaged to Suraj's phone.

*"All done guys!"* shouted Suraj, *"The flight is at 8:20am tomorrow and will arrive at Delhi at 11:05am. The cab driver will be waiting to take us to Rishikesh. It's a six-hour drive and we should arrive there by 6pm,"* said Suraj. *"Well, let's make tonight a night to remember then,"* said Nelson.

They went club hopping and returned to their hotel at 5am. Everyone had a quick shower to get rid of the foul club smell and having packed their bags, they headed for the airport. After their check-in, they sat in one of the restaurants for some breakfast.

*"No one disturb me on the flight please. I need to sleep, otherwise I'll be all moody and grumpy throughout the day,"* said Eloa. *"Me too!"* Exclaimed Nelson and Asher in chorus. Everyone was tired and slept the entire three hours on the flight.

At the arrival, a man was standing with Suraj's name on a placard. As soon as Suraj waved to him he came running and quickly took over the baggage trolley. They followed him to the car park. The weather was cool in Delhi as they sat in the SUV and hit the road.

Still tired and sleepy, they all fell asleep in the car. The road was smooth and straight for most of the part. *"Bhai (brother), please wake us up about half an hour before we reach,"* said Suraj tapping the shoulder of the driver.

Just when they were about half an hour away, the driver stopped at a popular *dhaba* (roadside restaurant) for some tea. He woke everyone up and they all visited the washroom to splash some water on their face and freshen up a little. They all had some hot tea with biscuits before getting into the car.

*"Just another twenty minutes and we'll be home,"* said Suraj as the others looked out the windows at the vast landscape and hills. Further on as they passed through the city towards the bungalow, Nelson could see many foreigners shopping, many wearing t-shirts and dresses that had images of different Indian gods and goddesses on them.

The driver took a sharp bend that led to a single lane road leading up a slope to some bungalows. The watchman opened the gates and as they drove in, one of the bungalows had a huge gathering outside it. It was decorated with flowers all over. A buffet had been laid out and many people seemed to be having a party.

A small boy who was playing near the gates noticed the car and ran in front it towards the bungalow shouting, *"They're here, they're here,"* and immediately a band of musicians in uniform, with huge trumpets, *dhols* (large drums) and trombones started playing some loud music.

People started dancing and cheering, coming towards the car as the driver parked just a little away from the bungalow. *"Dad has organized a party already,"* said Suraj shaking his head as they got out of the car. Nelson, Eloa and Asher were amused by what was going on.

An old man in his late sixties wearing a *kurta pajama* (traditional clothes) came towards the car. *"Dad,"* said Suraj as he went up to him, touched his feet and hugged him for a good minute or two. Everyone gathered around them, as Suraj touched the feet of his mother who looked graceful in a red *sari.*

Just then a small girl came up, *"Suraj bhaiya (brother), can I perform aarti for you and your friends?"* she asked with the sweetest smile. *"Of course you can,"* replied Suraj, *"This is an auspicious ritual to welcome guests,"* explained Suraj to his three friends as they stood still and let the pretty little girl do her thing.

She had a little *pooja thali* (steel plate), with *sindoor*, Indian sweets, rice grains and a *diya* (oil lamp). She put a red dot of *sindoor* on the forehead of the four of them, waved the plate clockwise around their faces a few times while ringing a tiny bell and reciting some prayers. She then fed each of them a piece of Indian sweets and said, *"Welcome home."*

Immediately after that some boys pulled Suraj to the center of the lawn and they started dancing to what the band was playing. Nelson, Eloa and Asher joined them all and this went on for a good twenty minutes during which elderly people came towards them and waved some money around their heads and gave it to the band members.

A little later Suraj's father signaled the band to stop and that's when Nelson, Eloa and Asher came to know that Suraj's father had invited all their close family and friends to welcome their son home after two years.

*"This is an awesome welcome!"* Exclaimed Eloa, *"The best reception I've ever gotten in my life,"* added Nelson. *"Parents get really excited when their children return from overseas. Apart from that they just need an excuse to gather everyone and have a party,"* said Suraj.

*"In India families need the smallest excuse to get together and celebrate. You'll find Christians celebrating Eid. Muslims celebrating Diwali and Hindus celebrating Christmas all together,"* replied Suraj as all the relatives came over to introduce themselves to Nelson, Eloa and Asher.

*"Hello, I am Rajesh, Suraj's maternal uncle. I have looked after Suraj from the time he was wearing nappies. He was a very naughty little boy and always wet my clothes whenever I picked him up,"* said an old jolly man with white beard and a broad smile on his face. *"Rajesh uncle, that's enough information. They're all part of our band and I have to go back to California to complete my Masters with them,"* interrupted Suraj pulling the old man aside.

Nelson, Eloa and Asher really enjoyed meeting everyone. They all seemed so friendly and happy to see them. The younger boys and girls had their phones out and were taking selfie photos with them. Foreigners are always given great hospitality in India and the local children love to show off their pictures with them.

It seemed like the neighbors had also been invited and the party carried on for about an hour more outside the house. They all sat on the chairs laid out in front of the house relishing the buffet that had been laid out.

It was past 7pm and getting dark. Slowly everyone started leaving and soon only Suraj's parents and the four of them were left behind.

Suraj's father pulled out a bundle of notes from his pocket and handed some of it to the musicians, the caterer and the decorator. Within minutes, the place was cleared of all the chairs, tables and utensils. Only the flowers on the door and a, *'Welcome Home'* sign was left behind.

*"That was awesome, thank you so much. Asante sana,"* said Asher as they all went into the bungalow. The main door opened into a huge sitting and dining area on the ground floor. A houseboy was laying dinner on a round glass dining table.

They all took a seat on the sofa chairs and had a long chat. They spoke about their concert, their travel, their music videos and studies at the University. It was past 9pm when they all decided to get some sleep. After dinner Suraj took them upstairs to the first floor. *"Asher this is your room. Mine is right opposite yours and my parents have the one next to mine,"* said Suraj as he opened one of the three bedroom doors on the first floor.

*"Let's go up to the terrace,"* said Suraj and they all followed him up the stairs. The door opened to the roof. Suraj switched on the terrace lights revealing a beautiful marble floored terrace that had a table-tennis table on the right side. A short wall went all around the rooftop. At the front left corner was a small cozy room.

Suraj opened the lock and let Nelson and Eloa put their bags in. It was a small but nice little bedroom with attached bathroom. Dim lights, some candlesticks on a side table and a tall dressing table on the side.

*"It's lovely Suraj! This is so beautiful,"* gasped Eloa. *"Come outside and let's sit for sometime,"* said Suraj. They went out and stood on the edge of the wall from where they could see the sacred Ganges River, the lights in the city were still on and many people were walking about. It had a beautiful view of the city and the Ganges.

*"Look up,"* said Suraj. *"Oh my God! It's a blanket of stars. Is this the house you grew up in?"* asked Nelson looking at Suraj. *"Yes it is. In the summers when it gets really hot, we'd sleep up here on the terrace facing the stars, wondering what went on, on the other planets and galaxies,"* said Suraj. *"This was my play area with my friends and cousins when they came over. Lots of memories on this rooftop,"* said Suraj.

*"I'm glad you like it. Tomorrow morning let's be up and ready by 9am. After breakfast we'll head into the city,"* announced Suraj as they all went into their respective rooms and hit the sack.

# RISHIKESH

The next morning everyone was up early and out of the house by 9am. They walked down the little slope and into the market area. Rishikesh had little shops in every nook and corner on the narrow streets. They walked through the shops to one of the most popular landmarks known as the *Laxman Jhula,* an iron bridge that connected the villages on both sides of the Ganges River.

A very narrow road led up to the *Laxman Jhula.* Cars couldn't go beyond a certain point and everyone was either walking, cycling or on motorbikes. It was a bright sunny morning and the town had already come alive with so many people around the place. The riverbanks of the Ganges River had many ashrams, ancient temples, hotels and restaurants on both sides.

There were plenty of western tourists who seemed to be very interested in spiritual activities. Some had beads around their necks and wrists; others had the same red *sindoor* dot on their foreheads while some were chanting out mantras loudly as they danced.

Most of the shops on both sides of the Ganges River sold spiritual books, spiritual music CDs, Indian traditional wear and yoga accessories. It was a market of spirituality. Every second signboard was either about a spiritual retreat, Vedanta classes, yoga workshops or meditation camps.

As they walked through the shops and over the bridge, they stood at the center of it looking at the river flowing below them and the green hills from where the river came down. It was a beautiful sight. They could also see another similar bridge a little ahead from where they were, that was called *Ram Jhula.*

*"So what are we doing today?"* asked Eloa. *"Well, we can look around the shops today, see if you would like to buy anything. They have very nice jewelry and clothes. The spiritual CDs they sell here have some awesome music and vocals on them. There's always a band or two playing somewhere that we can just sit and listen to. Apart from that if you're into anything like astrology, numerology, gemology or want check out the yoga and meditation studios, we can do that too,"* said Suraj.

*"After that we can go up the hill and sit at one of the popular restaurants and have lunch with a top view of the whole place,"* added Suraj. *"Yes, I'd definitely like to check out the yoga studios here,"* replied Eloa. *"I'd like to get some knowledge about the local culture and history of the place. Judging by the number of western tourists here, there must be something special about the place,"* said Asher.

As they kept walking Nelson walked into one of the bookshops. *"Hello there,"* said a middle-aged man behind the counter. He had hundreds of books neatly stacked up behind him. *"Hi, can you show me what the tourists come to Rishikesh for. What kind of books do they mostly buy from you?"* asked Nelson.

*"Many tourists come here to attain Spiritual Enlightenment and learn about God and the Ultimate Reality while others come to have a dip in the Holy Ganges River. Many others come here to do 'seva' (selfless work), and because there are many spiritual gurus around, often tourists come over to have their 'darshan' (seeing and hearing from them in person),"* said the man, in an Indian accent.

*"What was the third thing you mentioned after Spiritual Enlightenment and God?"* asked Asher. *"The Ultimate Reality,"* replied the man. *"Yes, what is that?"* asked Asher.

"It's what the Upanishads call 'Brahman' and it is the Absolute Truth about God, the Universe, and you," came the reply. "I've never heard of that before, have you?" asked Asher looking at Nelson. "Nope! What are the Upanishads?" asked Nelson and the man quickly pulled out over fifteen books and placed the on the counter.

"The Upanishads contain the highest knowledge about the Absolute Reality, Brahman. They are in the form of short profound stories that are found in the four Vedas. These are a few of the popular ones," said the man holding up the books.

"Let's go, we're getting late. Uncle, we'll come back later," said Suraj looking at the man and pulling Nelson and Asher out of the shop. "Late? Late for what?" asked Asher once they were outside. "You have to be careful with these shopkeepers. This one would have easily sold you at least 4-5 books that you don't need and would never read. The people behind the counters here will say anything to make a sale," said Suraj as they walked on.

Eloa saw a fancy looking yoga studio and headed towards it. "You go and check it out, we'll wait outside," said Nelson as she went in. "No seriously, what was that guy talking about? What Ultimate truth is there of God, the Universe and us? What was the word he mentioned?" asked Nelson. "Brahman," replied Suraj. "You know about it?" asked Asher.

*"Yes I've heard about it since my childhood. Very few Saints and enlightened people claim to have realized it but I would say ninety-nine percent of the people that try to realize it usually fail and give up in no time. Don't waste your time on it. And besides that, all these enlightened people are a bore. We're still young and should enjoy life. You don't want to become a boring monk who gives up all his possessions and then begs for his food everyday do you?"* asked Suraj looking at both Nelson and Asher.

*"No of course not,"* replied Asher shaking his head. Eloa was back with a smile. *"They have some awesome yoga teachers here, very friendly and the prices are very cheap compared to California,"* said Eloa. *"Maybe I'll join for a few sessions while we're in Rishikesh,"* she said, winking at Nelson.

They carried on walking through the streets and the boys tried on different t-shirts and outfits that no one would dare to wear in California. All the Indian gods and goddesses have one thing in common; they're all very colorful. Nelson picked up a blue t-shirt with Lord Shiva on it just because it looked *cool*. He had no idea who Lord Shiva is.

Eloa bought some nice stone earrings, bangles and bracelets. She loved the cute anklets that most of the young girls walking around were wearing. She bought some for herself and some to take back for her friends.

Suraj showed them most of the places where he grew up in. On the weekends all the boys got together to play gully cricket with a tennis ball. He took them to his nursery and primary school and the park that they went to after bunking school and finally his favorite eating spots.

They landed back near the *Laxman Jhula* and Suraj led them into a lovely little restaurant called *'The Little Buddha Cafe'* that was on the riverbank and had two floors of seating area with an open view of the River Ganges.

They climbed the steps to the top seating area for a better view and occupied a table right on the edge of the wooden platform. The place was full of foreigners and the menu offered Oriental, American, European, Mediterranean and Indian cuisine.

They pulled up some chairs and sat facing the river and city on the opposite side. They had a great view of the temples on both sides of the riverbank. They could hear bells being rung in the temples and mantras being sung on the loudspeakers from where they were seated.

*"This is one of my favorite restaurants. It has a great view and the owner is a family friend. He knows what I love and we also get a good discount. Take a look at the menu. Everything on it is awesome, you can order any of the items,"* said Suraj confidently.

*"I need to find out what this Brahman thing is. It's stuck in my head now. It's going to bother me until I know what it is,"* said Nelson looking at Suraj. They gave the waiter their orders. *"I'm telling you, forget about it. It's all very boring and besides, are you looking to get spiritually enlightened?" "No, of course not!"* Exclaimed Nelson, *"I'm not into all this enlightenment thing but I'd like to know what it is that they're teaching and talking about that's all,"* said Nelson.

They enjoyed the view and the cool breeze that was blowing across the restaurant. The gushing sound of the water flowing rapidly added to the ambience. As Suraj had said, the food was really delicious and they sat for about an hour more just talking about their next single, college life and what to do in the remaining days in India.

As the sun was setting, they left the place and Suraj led them to *Triveni Ghat*, one of the most popular tourist attractions in Rishikesh. Triveni Ghat is a part of the Ganga River bank where pilgrims take a dip in the Holy River. Everyday at sunset priests perform the grand *aarti* (prayer) to the sacred river. It is a sight to see with thousands of devotees and tourists flocking there every evening to be a part of it.

Almost over twenty priests holding great sacred oil lamps known as *diyas* waved them in circles facing the river as a group of people sang some prayers. Huge drums were played and conch shells were blown. The prayers went on for almost half an hour. Next to the river, many people were lighting their own *diyas* (small clay oil lamps) and leaving them to float on the river. The whole event of sound and light was simply unforgettable.

The river was filled with hundreds of such *diyas* making it a beautiful sight to see and experience. After that they slowly walked back towards their bungalow. The city was still buzzing with activity, the streetlights were on; some beggars were looking for food while many tourists made way to different places for dinner and to meet other like-minded travelers.

*"Tonight we'll have dinner at home. Mom is a great cook and she said to make sure we're back by dinnertime,"* said Suraj, as they slowly walked up the slope, through the gates, greeting the watchman and into the bungalow. Suraj's mother was indeed a great cook and she had prepared a full three course Indian meal that was followed by ice cream and cake for dessert.

"Uncle, do you know what Brahman is?" asked Nelson looking at Suraj's father who looked surprised, "Not really Nelson, but why do you ask?" came the reply. "I want to know what it is. We met a local shopkeeper who said it's the Ultimate Reality of God, the entire Universe and us. This has been bothering me since he mentioned it. I'm not looking to get enlightened or become a monk or a saint, but I need to know what it is that qualifies to be called the Ultimate Reality," said Nelson.

"Well if you're really interested in learning about it, you'll have to go to someone who knows the ancient scriptures well enough to explain it perfectly without a glitch, and someone who can clear all the doubts and questions that will arise. Suraj, take Nelson to meet Dinesh Acharya tomorrow morning. I'll call him right away and let him know that you'll be coming to see him."

"He's our family friend and usually advises us during cultural and religious functions and rituals. He is very well versed with the Vedas and Upanishads. He's your best bet because in Rishikesh one has to be careful of fake gurus who will con you out of all your money and possessions," said Suraj's father as he dialed a number on his mobile phone and walked into the balcony.

*"How could I forget Dinesh Acharya?"* said Suraj, *"It's been ages since I met him. He is the most respected acharya around (Acharya is a title given to a scholar of spiritual scriptures). He does have a lot of knowledge about our ancient scriptures,"* said Suraj, as his father walked back in. *"Suraj, make sure you're at Laxman Jhula by 10am. Ramu will meet you there and escort you to the village where he is taking his classes this week. You do remember Ramu, don't you?"* asked his father, *"Yes I do and don't worry dad, we'll be there on time,"* replied Suraj.

They all wished Suraj's parents a goodnight and went upstairs onto the terrace. The houseboy brought them a steaming teapot with some cups and some cookies. They sat for a couple of hours talking, laughing and singing a little before calling it a night.

Nelson searched for the word *Brahman* on the Internet and read a few of the posts available but none made sense to him. *"We'll find out tomorrow I guess,"* he said looking at Eloa as she put off the lights and snuggled up to him.

## DINESH ACHARYA

Next morning they were all up early and walked to the *Laxman Jhula*. Ramu was Dinesh Acharya's son who was around twelve years old. He loved coming to play at Suraj's house when Dinesh Acharya visited them. Suraj remembered giving away his old school books to Ramu every year after he had graduated to the next class. Ramu was already there and Suraj introduced him to his friends.

*"We must hurry, it will take about half an hour to reach there. Father will be waiting for us. He has cancelled his class today to meet you all,"* said Ramu.

He led them through and out of the city. They walked through a small jungle and into another village. *"This is Achintya Village. Achintya means 'unthinkable' and is also another name of Lord Shiva,"* said Ramu as they walked through the narrow lanes between a few houses before turning into one of them that had a signboard outside that read:

### *"Free Vedanta Classes*
### *With Dinesh Acharya."*

They walked into what was a classroom with wooden chairs and desks facing a blackboard. An old man wearing round glasses and old tattered clothes sat at the teacher's table holding a book. He was so engrossed in what he was reading that he didn't notice Ramu and the rest walk in.

*"Father, Suraj and his friends are here,"* said Ramu going up to the front. The old man looked up above his reading glasses and motioned them to have a seat. After a few seconds he closed the book he was reading and got up, *"How are you doing Suraj? How are your studies going on in USA? Are they teaching you anything worthwhile?"* asked Dinesh Acharya looking at Suraj and then at everyone else.

*"Namaste uncle, I'm fine, yes my studies are going on well. These are my friends from the same University. This is Nelson, Asher and Eloa. They're very intrigued about our culture, and Nelson in particular wants to know what Brahman is. Dad said to meet you as you would be the best person who can explain it to us,"* said Suraj as they all sat on some chairs.

*"Brahman is not something that can be known,"* replied Dinesh as he got up and sat on the table facing them all. *"Will that be all?"* he asked looking at their surprised faces. *"Why can't it be known uncle?"* asked Nelson looking a little startled. *"You may address me as Acharya-ji, not uncle. The least you can do for a teacher is to give him some respect,"* replied Dineshji in a sweet voice not sounding angry or irritated at all.

*"Okay Acharyaji, what do you teach to your students if Brahman cannot be known?"* asked Nelson. *"I teach Advaita Vedanta which is non-duality,"* replied Dineshji with a slight smile. *"And what is Advaita Vedanta about?"* asked Nelson.

*"Oh, Advaita Vedanta is about Brahman,"* came the reply. *"What? You just said it can't be known, but you teach about it?"* asked Asher looking confused. *"That's right. I teach about Brahman, but it can't be known,"* replied Dineshji.

*"Acharyaji, please teach me about Brahman, and leave the 'knowing' of Brahman part to me. I'm quite good with intellectual studies, understanding concepts and philosophies,"* replied Nelson sounding a little over confident.

*"So you think you are clever huh? What have you learnt so far?"* asked Dineshji. *"I'm quite intelligent and have always been the topper in all my school and college years. I have a much higher IQ level than most people. You can ask me anything,"* said Nelson looking at Dineshji.

*"Really?"* asked Dineshji looking sternly at Nelson, *"Well in that case I'll just ask you one question,"* said Dineshji. *"Sure,"* replied Nelson. *"Do you know that, by knowing which, everything is known?"* asked Dinesh. *"What!"* Exclaimed everyone at once looking at Dineshji like they hadn't heard him correctly.

*"Do you know that, by knowing which, everything is known?"* repeated Dineshji. *"Is that even possible?"* asked Nelson. *"Absolutely! And that is what the Upanishads and Advaita Vedanta are about. That is Brahman! That is what I teach. Look at the chair you're sitting on, what is it made of?"* asked Dineshji. *"Wood,"* replied Asher. *"You know what wood is?"* asked Dineshji looking at Asher. *Of course! It's the material or the substance that this chair is made of,"* replied Asher.

*"What is my chair made of?"* asked Dineshji, pointing to the chair behind his table. *"Wood!"* replied Eloa. *"Okay, I'm sure you know that all the chairs here are made of wood,"* said Dineshji. *"Yes,"* came a unanimous reply. *"That's good. What about a similar chair in Europe, Africa, Australia or America? What would they all be made of?"* asked Dineshji, *"WOOD!!!"* Shouted everyone in unison looking surprised.

*"So a wooden chair made in any part of the world is made of wood. Would there not be any differences in all those chairs?"* asked Dineshji looking at everyone.

*"Of course there will be many differences,"* replied Asher, *"The chairs will have different shapes, sizes, uses, strengths, weaknesses and names,"* replied Nelson looking at Dineshji.

*"That's a great answer. So that means that wooden chairs in any part of the world are made of the same material or substance called 'wood' but have different names, forms and uses. I'd like you to apply that logic to every object made of wood, in every part of the world, whether it is a cupboard, table, door, house, pencils, stools, boats, paper, cardboard, beds, benches and so on. Can you do that?"* asked Dinesh looking for confirmation.

*"So, what you're trying to say is that any wooden object in any part of the world is made of the same material or substance called wood but the only difference in all those objects is in their shapes, sizes, uses, strengths, weaknesses and names. Is that what you're saying?"* asked Nelson looking at Dineshji.

*"You certainly have a higher IQ level than most people,"* replied Dinesh with a sly smile. *"That is half of what I'm saying, but a good start nevertheless. What is important here is that by knowing what 'wood' is, you know the cause of any and every 'wooden' object in the world. The objects WILL have different shapes, sizes, uses, strengths, weaknesses and names BUT their material cause or substance is ONE AND THE SAME!"* said Dineshji.

*"So what you're saying is that in the same way that wood is known to be the substance or substratum of every wooden object in the world, there's something that we can know which would be the substance or substratum of the entire Universe? Is that what you're saying?"* asked Nelson sounding excited.

*"Yes my boy! Wood is the substratum of all wooden objects, and in the same way there's something that's the substratum of everything in the Universe,"* replied Dineshji.

*"Now that is something that sounds worth learning. Acharyaji, please teach us that because I don't think they teach that in any University. On the other hand I don't think anything like that exists. If there were, it would be the only thing schools would ever teach children. Come on Acharyaji, you've got my full attention now. I need to hear about this. But please if this is a prank or something that's not true, we can stop right now, as I have a very bad temper that I wouldn't want to lose on you,"* said Nelson.

*"Ha ha ha,"* laughed Dineshji loudly, *"I wouldn't want that too. And I am serious only if you are. I will need you to attend at least six classes to share this profound wisdom,"* replied Dineshji. *"Done deal. Acharyaji, I'm a very intellectual and learned guy so if you're going to ask me to accept anything based on your religion, blind faith or personal beliefs we can stop right now,"* said Nelson.

*"And if you are about to state that God is everything and that by knowing God I will know everything, we can stop right now, because no one has seen God and if someone claims to have seen God, they can't prove it to anyone else. So, unless you're going to show me God and prove that He or She is everything, we can stop right now,"* said Nelson giving Dineshji a serious look.

*"My child, I'm not talking about God, I'm talking about something much higher than that,"* said Dineshji. *"What?"* Exclaimed everyone *"Higher than God? Nothing is higher than God,"* said Eloa. *"That's exactly what I'm taking about,"* replied Dineshji. *"I don't understand Acharyaji,"* said Nelson looking confused.

*"Since you're an intelligent boy I ask you to keep your mind open and not restrict yourself to what you have learnt and known all your life. You are free to, and I would encourage you to question and clear the slightest doubts that arise as I talk, but once you find it logical, I ask you to accept it as being the Absolute Truth,"* said Dineshji.

*"Okay, so, by knowing what does one know everything in the Universe?"* asked Nelson looking at Dineshji. *"Okay, so here we go. The reality of the entire Universe is 'Brahman'. It's a term given to the reality of this Universe. You can call it whatever you like. I'll use the term Brahman because the Upanishads call it that. Brahman is infinite Pure Existence and Pure Consciousness,"* said Dineshji.

*"If Brahman is the 'reality' as you just said, that means that there must be something that is 'unreal' as well, right?"* interrupted Asher. *"Yes, the Universe as we see it is unreal,"* replied Dineshji. *"Really? So this classroom is not real, these chairs are not real, the trees and mountains outside are not real. The Sun, moon and stars are not real?"* asked Eloa.

*"Precisely! Let me explain what Vedanta means by 'real', which will make it clear. By 'real', Vedanta means that which is true in all places, at all times and in all things. Anything that depends on a particular time, space or object to exist is termed as 'unreal' or 'false'. This chair is here and not outside, it was made and will be destroyed and is only this chair and not anything else."*

*"This chair is true here but false outside. It became true as a chair when it was made and if we break it or burn it, it will no longer be a chair. Also it is true as only this chair and not any other thing. We can't term it as being 'real' because it is limited in time, space and object identity."*

*"But Brahman is not limited in any way at all. In fact, every thing or object in the Universe is limited in time, space and object identity but Brahman is limitless in all three,"* said Dineshji.

*"So what you're saying is that Brahman is the reality of the Universe. We know that every thing put together is the Universe. So from what I've grasped so far, Brahman is the reality of the Universe and all the things in the Universe are limited in time, space and object identity, am I right?"* asked Nelson. *"Yes,"* replied Dineshji.

*"So, everything in the Universe is limited or finite, but the reality of all these finite things, Brahman, is infinite. Is this correct too?"* asked Nelson. *"Yes,"* replied Dineshji.

*"Let me get this straight; all 'things' or 'objects' are finite and Brahman is infinite so Brahman cannot be a 'thing' or 'object', right?"* *"Yes,"* replied Dineshji.

*"Brahman is not an 'object' or a 'thing'. And yet it is the reality of all things?"* *"Yes!"* Exclaimed Dineshji raising his eyebrows and surprised at the questions that Nelson was firing at him.

*"A thing can be known or unknown to me, you or anyone else but because Brahman is not a thing it cannot be known, am I right?"* asked Nelson. *"Absolutely correct! Things are known by using your mind but Brahman cannot be known by the mind. But don't think it is unknown because it is the most known,"* replied Dineshji.

*"You're contradicting yourself here. Brahman cannot be known yet it is the most known? That's completely paradoxical,"* argued Nelson. *"Correct! In fact, all paradoxes can be used to refer to Brahman such as; it is nearer than the nearest and further than the furthest. It is smaller than the smallest and larger than the largest. It is not a thing yet every thing is it and so on,"* replied Dineshji.

*"So, if I understand Brahman,"* said Nelson. *"You cannot understand Brahman,"* interrupted Dineshji. *"Okay Acharyaji, then what is it that you can teach us if Brahman cannot be understood?"* asked Nelson. *"I will teach you what it is not,"* came the reply. *"How will that help?"* asked Eloa. *"Well, after you have understood everything that it is not, what remains is Brahman,"* replied Dineshji looking at their blank faces.

*"I'm still not sure of what you're saying but I'll let you carry on Acharyaji,"* said Nelson. *"Thank you my boy. As I was saying, Brahman is the reality of every thing in the Universe, and every thing in the Universe that we know or perceive is unreal because it is limited in time, space and object identity. Brahman "appears" as the Universe due to limitations in time, space and object identity,"* said Dineshji.

*"So in reality, the Universe that we see and perceive is nothing but Brahman?"* interrupted Asher. *"That is correct!"* Exclaimed Dineshji. *"So how does Brahman "appear" as the Universe?"* asked everyone in unison.

41

*"Brahman by it's own inherent power called 'Maya' projects and veils Brahman to appear as the Universe,"* replied Dineshji. *"What is Maya? And how does it work?"* asked Nelson.

*"Like I said, Maya is the inherent power of Brahman and it makes Brahman 'appear' as the Universe by 'projecting' and 'veiling' Brahman. Let me explain,"* said Dineshji. *"Please do,"* replied Asher instantly.

*"Maya is not a separate quality or separate power of Brahman, it is Brahman's inherent power. Maya does two things to Brahman. It projects Brahman and it veils or covers Brahman. By doing so, Brahman as the Universe seems external and separate from you, and is known by different names, forms and objects."*

*"Brahman is non-dual, there's no internal or external in Brahman. When Maya projects Brahman, then Brahman appears to be both internal and external. At this point there is you and the entire Universe 'outside' you. Using names and forms Brahman is veiled or covered so that you don't perceive Brahman, but instead you perceive names and forms. Thus every thing has a name, form and use."*

*"Brahman is formless but Maya makes it 'appear' in different forms. Brahman is infinite but Maya makes it 'appear' to be finite by limiting these forms in time, space and object identity. Brahman is one without a second (non-dual), but Maya makes it 'appear' as many. Brahman is ever unchanging but Maya makes it 'appear' as*

*constantly changing. Thus the Universe "appears" to exist in the reality of Brahman."*

*"What or who are you in this entire Universe?"* asked Dineshji, before answering it himself. *"You are known as a 'jiva'. Jiva is the individual sentient person who perceives the Universe outside him or her. So now, we have Brahman, Maya and Jiva. The reality (Brahman), the appearance (Maya) and you (Jiva)! For now whenever I say 'you' it refers to the person that you think you are, or your ego,"* said Dineshji looking to confirm that they all understood what he was saying. *"Ok, but what else can it refer to?"* asked Eloa looking surprised. *"Oh, that will come later. Let's understand the reality, what is perceived and you, for now,"* said Dineshji.

*"Let me try and summarize,"* said Nelson scratching his head. *"There's one reality called Brahman which is infinite Pure Existence and Pure Consciousness. Brahman with its own inherent power called Maya projects and veils Brahman to appear as the Universe. Maya makes Brahman appear as either here or there (Space), before or after (Time) and this or that (Object Identity). Maya limits Brahman in space, time and objects and thus the Universe 'appears' to exist,"* said Nelson. *"Brilliant!"* Exclaimed Dineshji.

*"What about me and you and everybody else?"* asked Nelson. *"You are Brahman! You are the Absolute Reality. You as Brahman project this entire Universe with your inherent power called Maya. This entire creation including the person*

43

*that you think you are 'appears' in you, Brahman,"* said Dineshji.

*"Ha ha ha. And I am God,"* said Suraj laughing out loud. *"If there is only one reality of the entire Universe and it is me then what about you and the other people around?"* asked Asher. *"There is only one reality in which every thing and every body appears. The person that you are, and that we all think we are, all appear in that one reality. There is only one real identity which is Brahman, which is you,"* said Dineshji.

*"Great! If you can convince me philosophically and logically that All-is-One, that would be awesome because we've all heard it before but no one has ever proven it to anyone ever,"* said Nelson looking at the rest of them.

*"I can give you some examples that would help you intellectually understand what Brahman is like,"* said Dineshji. *"And that's all we need! We're all A-grade students, just give us the foundation and we'll do the rest,"* said Nelson. Dineshji looked at them with a sly smile.

*"Like I said, you will all need to attend six classes at least. I'm here in Achintya Village for this entire week but I don't have many students here so you can attend everyday for the next six days. All I ask is for you to be serious about learning and not missing a class. If you're on, we can start from tomorrow morning. Be here by 9am,"* said Dineshji as he got up from the table and went back to the book he was reading.

Suraj and everyone left the place and walked back through the little jungle towards the city. It was past lunchtime and Suraj took them to a fast food riverside restaurant where they enjoyed some *veg biryani* and *steamy masala dosas*. On the way back home, Nelson spotted a bicycle hiring shop and they hired four mountain bikes for the next six days. *"It would be adventurous to explore the city on a bike and we'll save time walking to Achintya Village in the mornings,"* said Nelson, as they all rode home.

*"Did you get what he was saying? I am completely confused. Hey? Mr. Intelligent?"* asked Eloa pinching Nelson on the arm as they sat on the terrace underneath the stars after dinner. *"Of course I got what he was saying,"* replied Nelson looking at everyone's surprised faces.

*"Well, he said there is one entity called Brahman. Brahman is not a thing or an object. This Brahman has a power that projects itself to manifest as this entire Universe. He mentioned people as well. So everybody including all of us here are things or objects to Brahman. He also said that our real identity is Brahman, which means our current identity is unreal or false."*

*"Brahman is the Subject to all the objects in the Universe including the person that we think we are. The Subject to every thing cannot be a thing itself. 'I' am the Subject to the entire Universe and there is only one Universal 'I'. We are not separate as we currently think ourselves to be,"* replied Nelson.

*"What? How did you get that from all the confusing stuff he said?"* blurted Eloa. *"That's the difference between an A-grade student and an average student,"* said Nelson pinching back Eloa with a chuckle. *"So you now think you are God?"* asked Eloa slapping him on his back.

*"I get what you just said but how is it possible? It goes against everything we know and life in general,"* said Asher looking at Nelson. *"I know what you mean but the solution would be very simple if we knew ourselves as Brahman, which we don't. Dineshji did say he would explain to us what Brahman is 'like'. If we understand that, it may be possible to realize ourselves Brahman,"* said Nelson.

*"But how can one thing be everything?"* asked Eloa. *"It is not a thing!"* Exclaimed Nelson. *"Okay if it's not a thing then what is it?"* asked Eloa. *"It is the one 'Subject' to which everything in the Universe is an 'object' or 'thing'. Let me put it simple words for all of you,"* said Nelson. *"That's my boy. There's a reason I'm dating you,"* said Eloa with smile.

*"Just understand this for now. The underlying reality of everything in the Universe is Brahman and you are that reality. What you currently know as the Universe and yourselves is false or unreal. Now Acharyaji needs to explain how Brahman is everything and everybody. Got it?"* asked Nelson. *"Hmmm. Interesting. We'll find out tomorrow,"* said Asher as they all dispersed to their rooms.

# CLAY AND POT

The next morning, everyone got up early and after breakfast they cycled their way to *Achintya Village* reaching there in fifteen minutes flat. *"You guys do the talking and I'll take down notes which we can refer to later. And don't worry if it's boring, I've planned for some adventurous and exciting places to visit after the classes. You need to experience the real Rishikesh as well,"* said Suraj as they walked into the classroom. Dineshji was already waiting for them.

*"You're six minutes late,"* said Dineshji looking at his watch, *"Make sure you're not late for the remaining days,"* he said very politely. *"Yes Acharyaji, we'll ensure we reach on or before time from tomorrow,"* replied Suraj who was really not interested in this whole Brahman thing but came along with rest anyway.

Suraj had brought a notepad and pen with him. *"Great. We'll cover three major examples used in Vedanta first. These three examples explain what Brahman is 'like' compared to the Universe and you. We'll cover one example a day over three days and in the remaining three days we'll cover why the Universe 'appears' as we see it,"* said Dineshji as walked to the back of the classroom and pulled out a clay pot from an old cupboard and walked back to the front. He placed the pot on the table where everyone could see it.

*"The first example we'll cover today is that of the Clay and Pot. This is a Pot made of Clay,"* said Dineshji pointing towards the pot and looking at everyone who nodded their heads in the affirmative. *"Good. As I explain the example, feel free to ask any questions as and when they arise in your minds. You may interrupt me at anytime. I will cover this example in depth and that will take a little more time than the rest of the examples, so please bear with me."*

*"What do we have on the table?"* asked Dineshji *"A Pot!"* Exclaimed everyone together. *"Yes we have a pot. Is the pot real?"* asked Dineshji. *"We can all see it so it must be real,"* replied Eloa. *"Not a very clever answer but anyway, we think, feel and know that there is a thing or an object on the table that is called a 'pot'. It looks like a pot, is shaped like pot, can be used as a pot and is called a pot."*

48

*"Vedanta says you need to examine the pot to find out its reality. It says that what you are seeing on the table is NOT a pot,"* said Dineshji. *"Of course it's a pot, what else could it be?"* asked Asher looking confused. *"Let's examine it my dear,"* replied Dineshji.

*"The pot on the table is a 'thing', 'object' or an 'effect' like everything in the Universe. Every effect must have a cause. For example, the chairs you are sitting on are made of wood. Wood is the cause and chair is the effect. The chair exists because of wood. In the same way we have a pot, which is an 'object', 'thing' or an 'effect' of something. How and where can we find the cause of an effect?"*

*"Here's a good piece of advice. The cause of something is found in the effect itself. Like wood is found in the chair. To find the cause of anything examine the effect. So, now if we examine the pot to find its cause, we can clearly see that the pot is made of something called clay. Are you following me so far?"* asked Dineshji and everyone nodded their heads.

*"Great, remember, we first had a pot on the table and now we know that the material cause of the pot is clay. In the first look we had a pot. Now we have a pot made of clay. Does it sound logical and correct so far?"* asked Dineshji and they nodded their heads again.

*"Vedanta says, examine it further. First you said it's a pot, and now you say that it's a 'pot' made of 'clay'. You are now mentioning two things, pot and clay. Are both the pot and the clay real things? If we look closely at the pot, the inside is made of clay, the outside is made of clay, the top and the bottom is made of clay. In fact the entire pot is made of only clay. From the top to the bottom and the inside to the outside, it is nothing but clay. If all of it is clay, then where is the pot?"* asked Dineshji

*"It's on the table,"* answered Eloa looking confused. *"And where is the clay?"* asked Dineshji looking at Eloa. *"It's on the table,"* replied Eloa. *"Are there two things on the table? Is there a Pot and Clay?"* asked Dineshji. *"The pot is not different from clay. But we honestly can't say that we have two real things on the table,"* replied Nelson which seemed to please Dineshji.

*"Well answered Nelson. Two real things can be seen and experienced separately such as the chair is one thing and the table is another. We can see and experience them separately; the table doesn't depend on the chair for its existence and vice versa. Is this true of the pot and clay? Can we see or experience the clay and the pot separately?"* asked Dineshji.

*"No,"* came the unanimous reply. *"We know the cause of the pot is real, therefore the clay is definitely a 'real' substance. Is the same true of the pot? Clay can exist without the pot but the pot cannot exist without clay. This means that the pot 'depends' on clay for its existence. The 'pot' is not a real substance like the 'clay' is."*

*"So what is a pot and where is it?"* asked Dineshji. *"It's on the table, why do you keep asking that?"* asked Eloa innocently and everyone burst out laughing. *"Let me carry on. Please try to follow what I'm saying. The entire 'thing', 'object' or 'effect' that is sitting on this table is 'clay' yet we are calling it a 'pot' because it looks like a pot, it can be used as a pot and it is called a pot. Pot is a 'name' given to a particular 'form' and 'use' of clay."*

*"Pot is an 'appearance' of clay in a particular form for a particular use. Every 'thing' in the Universe is an object and has a name, form and use, and that is how we know what they are. But names, forms and uses are not 'real' things; they are 'appearances' of the material cause or substance that they're made of. The 'cause' is always 'real' and the 'effect' is only an 'appearance'. The wood is real while the chair is an appearance. In the same way the clay is real while the pot is an appearance. There is no new 'thing' created by clay."*

*"In fact we can say that the clay is 'appearing' as a pot. So now we have 'negated' the effect, thing or object called pot. There is no 'real' thing, object or effect called pot. The effect is illusory, false or unreal. Because there is no new thing created by clay we can conclude that clay is NOT the cause of the pot. The clay did not create a new thing and cannot be called a 'cause' of the pot."*

*"Clay loses its causality and we realize that the reality of the object, effect or thing on the table is nothing but clay. We started off by recognizing a pot on the table and through inquiry we realize that the pot is false or an appearance. The reality of what we have on the table is only clay. Any questions?"* asked Dineshji.

*"Can I summarize please?"* asked Nelson. *"I hope I understood it correctly. First we see a pot, secondly we realize the pot is made of something called clay. Thirdly we realize that there is no 'real' thing as pot, it is through and through clay, and finally we realize clay didn't cause anything at all. It was, is and will be only clay,"* said Nelson.

*"That was wonderful Nelson. Did we all get that?"* asked Dineshji looking at everyone else. *"Yes but still just kind of understood it,"* replied Eloa. *"Would you like some steps of understanding this?"* asked Dineshji. *"Yes please,"* they all replied in a chorus. *"Okay, there are just 4 Steps in this example using the law of cause and effect. Every 'thing' or 'object' has a cause, and every cause has an effect. Here they are,"* said Dineshji as he wrote on the blackboard.

### Step 1: The Thing or Effect
We start with a *'thing'* or *'effect'* called *'Pot'*.
(Pot = Effect)

### Step 2: The Cause Of The Effect
The cause is always found in the effect.
We check the *'Pot'* for its cause.
The *Pot* is made of one reality called *'Clay'*.
(Clay = Cause, Pot = Effect)

### Step 3: The 'Thing' Or 'Effect' Is Unreal
We check further and see that there is no such 'thing' as a 'Pot'. 'Pot' is only a *name* given to a specific *form* and *use* of *Clay*.
(Clay did not cause any new *'thing'* and *'Pot'* is only an *appearance* of *Clay*)

### Step 4: The Cause Loses Its Causality
The *effect* is unreal therefore Clay cannot be called a *cause*. Only Clay remains as the reality.
(Clay loses its causality)

"Okay but how does this relate to Brahman, the Universe and us?" asked Asher.

"In this example you are the Pot and Clay is Brahman," said Dineshji.

"You mean to say that we are all Pots and our reality is Clay. Is that correct?" asked Nelson.

"Absolutely correct. You are a Pot that has never heard of the word Clay and has no idea of what Clay is." "You have lived all your life in a Universe of different objects such as plates, statues, big pots and small pots, cups, jugs, bowls, lids and so on."

"They all have different shapes, sizes, forms, names and uses but they're all made of Clay. The small pot or the bowl or any of the items have never heard of clay. You think you are a Pot and every other item thinks that it is, what it is," said Dineshji.

"So basically it's a Universe of Clay items which all think and know themselves to be either a pot, bowl, plate, lid and so on. And they've never known or heard of Clay, just like we have never heard of Brahman and we think we are individual persons. Is that correct?" asked Asher.

*"That's a good way to look at it,"* said Dineshji looking at Asher. *"So, the Pot doesn't know it's true nature, it's true identity or it's reality. It desires to find out the truth about its origin or it's creator and thus seeks out an Acharya Pot to explain it to him,"* said Dineshji as he drew two pots on the blackboard and labeled them as Mr. Pot and Acharya Pot.

*"Let me write some equations that you can use for reference in the example. In your personal experience you know that you are an individual and that there is an entire Universe of things outside you and that there must be a Creator who created everything. The Individual, The Universe and The Creator. This our common experience. Vedanta says that You, the Universe and the Creator, is ONE and the SAME reality called Brahman,"* said Dineshji.

*"Now, in Mr. Pot's Universe we have Mr. Pot, millions of other items made of clay and a Creator that made up all these items. Thus there is the Mr. Pot, Mr. Pot's Universe and its Creator,"* said Dineshji.

## Example Equivalents:

**You = Mr. Pot**
**Your Universe = Mr. Pot's Universe**
***'Appears'* in Brahman = *'Appears'* in Clay**
***Brahman* Is Unknown = *Clay* Is Unknown**

**Your Identity = Individual Person**
**Mr. Pot's Identity = Individual Pot**
**Your True Identity = Brahman**
**Mr. Pot's True Identity = Clay**

**Spiritual Teacher = Acharya Pot**

*"Now, Mr. Pot and Acharya Pot are going to have a conversation and I want you to pay attention to what they say. I will talk on behalf of both of them,"* said Dineshji as he started.

*"Acharyaji, I would like to know the truth about myself, our Universe and its Creator. And secondly what happens when we are destroyed?"* asked Mr. Pot looking at Acharya Pot.

*"Mr. Pot, 'you' are the 'truth' of our Universe and its Creation. And 'you' are immortal. You were never created and can never be destroyed. In fact you are the underlying reality of everything that 'appears' as pots, plates, lids, bowls and so on,"* said the Acharya Pot.

*"How is that possible Acharyaji? I am only Mr. Pot. I am a small part of our Universe. I was made and will be destroyed one day. How can I be immortal? How can I be the reality of our entire Universe?"* asked Mr. Pot.

*"Mr. Pot, you have mistaken yourself to be a Pot. Your true identity is Clay,"* replied Acharya Pot. *"Clay? What is Clay?"* asked Mr. Pot. *"Clay is the smallest particle that you and everything in our Universe is made of. Look at yourself and imagine the smallest particle of you. That particle is called 'clay',"* said Acharya Pot.

(Some interesting information: Soil is made of three particles; Sand being the largest followed by Silt and then Clay. The clay particle is less than 0.002mm in diameter)

*"Oh, okay the smallest particle on my entire body would be too small to be seen by the naked eye, but I can imagine it to be the smallest existing brown particle. So that is what you are calling Clay right?"* asked Mr. Pot.

*"Yes, that particle is called Clay,"* replied Acharya Pot. *"Okay, I understand that I, as Mr. Pot, am made of Clay. I still don't understand how I am the entire Universe or immortal?"* asked Mr. Pot.

*"Great!"* Exclaimed Acharya Pot. *"Mr. Pot, you are made of Clay. Let's take a look inside you, around you and outside you. Look closely and you'll find that you are in fact made up entirely of Clay. There is nothing but Clay to Mr. Pot,"* said Acharya Pot.

Mr. Pot examined himself and declared, *"You're right Acharyaji. Everything that I know myself to be is made up of that Clay particle. There is no second thing apart from Clay. I am a Pot made of Clay. I understand that but how does that help?"* asked Mr. Pot.

*"Next let's examine to see if you really are Mr. Pot. Is there any reality to the Pot that you think you are, apart from the Clay? In fact look at all the items in our Universe, every particle of every thing is made of Clay,"* said Acharya Pot.

*"That's true, everything in our Universe is made of Clay but why do I still think, feel and know myself to be a Pot then?"* asked Mr. Pot. *"That's because this Pot has an individual 'clay-mind' that thinks, feels and knows itself to be a Pot. That clay-mind is attached to this Pot only and thus it knows itself to be limited to this Pot."*

*"Let's examine what a Pot is. If we take all the clay out of the Pot, will the Pot still exist?"* asked Acharya Pot. *"Of course not! If you take all the clay out of me I will be gone. Nothing of me will exist any longer,"* said Mr. Pot.

*"Will there still be a little outline of your shape or form if the clay is taken out?"* asked Acharya Pot. *"No! Every particle of me is made of Clay, there will be nothing left if all the Clay is taken out,"* replied Mr. Pot.

*"Will the Clay remain or still exist after it's taken out from the Pot?"* asked Acharya Pot. *"Yes, the clay can still exist in some form or another. Maybe as a lump of clay or broken pieces,"* replied Mr. Pot.

*"Clay can and will exist without Mr. Pot but Mr. Pot cannot exist without Clay. Do you agree?"* asked Acharya Pot. *"Yes it sounds correct. I cannot exist without Clay but Clay can exist without me. A Pot 'depends' on clay for its existence and not vice versa,"* said Mr. Pot.

*"So, the real substance, substratum or underlying reality of the Pot is Clay? There is no separate 'thing' or 'object' called Pot apart from Clay. Do you agree?"* asked Acharya Pot.

*"Yes, sounds correct. There is no 'thing' called Pot apart from Clay. But I still see you and me as a Pot. If we're both Clay then what is a Pot?"* asked Mr. Pot.

*"Great question. Let's examine from Clay's point of view. Where is clay in the Pot?"* asked Acharya Pot. *"It's in every particle of the Pot,"* replied Mr. Pot. *"If the Pot is destroyed and it's clay is remolded into a bowl, the same clay that was once the Pot will now be called a Bowl. Is that correct?"* asked Acharya Pot.

*"Yes. The Clay can be used to create something else,"* replied Mr. Pot. *"So Clay remains the same always but when it's form and shape changes, it is given a new name and use. Clay in the form of you and me is given the name 'Pot'. The same clay when remolded into that object is given the name 'Bowl',"* said Acharya Pot pointing to a Clay Bowl.

*"This means that Clay in different 'forms', used for different 'purposes' is given different 'names' and we call them 'things'. All these 'things' form our Universe. 'Things' are simply different forms, names and uses of Clay. The real substance, substratum or underlying reality of our Universe is 'Clay'. Every 'thing' that we know is only a particular form with a particular name and use,"* said Acharya Pot.

*"Agreed Acharyaji, what you are saying is accepted and logical BUT I still think, feel and know myself to be a Pot. Why is that?"* asked Mr. Pot. *"Your 'clay-mind' pervades this Pot only and so it perceives everything else as separate from it. Your life is experienced in your mind and your mind 'thinks' you are the body and the mind. This is a mistaken identity. You are neither the body nor the mind. You are Clay!"*

*"So your 'mind' has to realize that everything in our Universe is simply different names, forms and uses of Clay. Names, forms and uses are not real things. Clay in the form of a Pot 'appears' to be a Pot. Clay in the form of a Bowl 'appears' to be a Bowl. This is because there is no reality or substance called Pot or Bowl,"* said Acharya Pot.

Having enacted the above dialogue Dineshji looked at everyone, *"Did you get that? The Pot thinks it's a Pot. It then learns about Clay and realizes that the Pot is made of Clay. On further examination it realizes that there is no Pot without Clay. It looks around its Universe and sees everything made of nothing but Clay. Everything is Clay in different names, forms and uses. Names, forms and uses are unreal, only Clay is real."*

*"In the same way, you think you are a person. Then you learn about Brahman (Pure Existence and Consciousness) and realize that every particle of your body and mind is made of Brahman (Pure Existence and Consciousness). On further examination, you realize that there is no person without Brahman (Pure Existence and Consciousness). You look around the Universe and see that everything is made of nothing but Brahman (Pure Existence and Consciousness). Everything is Brahman in different names, forms and uses. Names, forms and uses are unreal, only Brahman (Pure Existence and Consciousness) is real,"* said Dineshji.

Nelson put his hand up, *"Acharyaji, what about the Potter or Creator who created all the clay items you mentioned. Where does he fit in?"* asked Nelson. *"I'm glad you asked that Nelson. It is the most common error made while trying to understand this example and other examples in Vedanta."*

*"Clay is equivalent to Brahman in this example. Brahman with it's own power called 'Maya' projects Brahman to 'appear' as everything in this Universe. There is no separate or external Creator apart from Brahman. Brahman alone projects itself to 'appear' as the Universe."*

*"Now, the same should be true of Clay and fortunately it is. Clay particles have a power of 'cohesion'. Cohesion is the power of sticking together of particles of the same substance, in this case the particle the clay particle. This power of cohesion enables different forms to emerge. Thus Clay with its 'own' power of 'cohesion' projects Clay to 'appear' as different forms with different names and uses."*

*"One particle of Clay is Clay. A million particles of Clay will 'form' a 'lump' of Clay. A few billion particles of Clay are shaped into a Bowl or a Pot. All these particles bind together because of the power of 'cohesion' of Clay particles. Regardless of how many Clay particles bind or stick together to form a 'thing' or 'object', the reality of the thing or object will be nothing apart from Clay."*

*"There is no external Potter assumed in this example because if a Potter would be introduced in the example to mold and create the pot, then Brahman would also require an external Creator or God to mold and create the Universe. The power of Brahman projects Brahman to 'appear' as different things. The power of Clay projects Clay to 'appear' as different things,"* explained Dineshji looking to see if everyone got it.

*"I got most of what you're trying to explain Acharyaji,"* replied Nelson while the rest of them still looked a little doubtful and not fully convinced.

*"Acharyaji, so what you're saying is that our true identity is Brahman (Pure Existence and Pure Consciousness) and everything in the Universe is not real but an appearance of Brahman?"* asked Nelson.

*"Yes Nelson. Just like all the things in the Universe of Clay are just different names, forms and uses of Clay, in the same way all the things in our Universe are just different names, forms and uses of Pure Existence and Consciousness. Brahman (Infinite Pure Existence and Consciousness) is the reality of the Universe. The Universe only 'appears' in Brahman,"* said Dineshji.

*"Keep in mind that Pot and Clay are both objects to us so it may be easier to understand what the clay and pot are, but when it comes to Brahman it seems a little confusing. This is because you are trying to objectify Brahman. Pure Existence is not a thing. Things exist because of Existence itself. Pure Consciousness is not a thing either. Things (Including our body and mind) are experienced because of Consciousness itself."*

*"Brahman's power of Maya projects a Universe that 'appears' to 'exist' and 'experience' itself (the appearance) through individual minds. Things exist and experience other things. Your body and mind are also things that exist and experience other things. Brahman, your true identity, does not exist; it is Existence itself. Brahman, your true identity, is not conscious; it is Consciousness itself."*

*"In the Universe of Clay-Things, Clay is the Absolute Reality. In The Universe of Existing-Things, Existence is the Absolute Reality. If the Pot realizes that everything is made of the clay particle and abides as clay, it becomes one with its entire Universe. Similarly if the person (you) realizes that 'everything exists in consciousness' and abides as consciousness, he or she becomes one with the entire Universe,"* said Dineshji picking up the pot and walking to the back of the classroom to put it back in the cupboard.

*"Let me write the same steps with regard our Universe and Brahman,"* said Dineshji as he walked towards the blackboard and wrote on it.

## Step 1: The Thing or Effect
We start with a *'thing'* or *'effect'* called *'Universe'*.
(Universe = Effect)

## Step 2: The Cause Of The Effect
The cause is always found in the effect.
We check the *'Universe'* for its cause.
The Universe is made *'things'* that *EXIST*.
We check *'things'* for their *cause*
*'Things'* or the *Universe* is made of one reality
called *Existence*. Things that *'exist'* make the
Universe. Without *Existence* itself there can be no
*thing* or *Universe.*
(Brahman = Cause, Universe = Effect)

## Step 3: The 'Thing' Or 'Effect' Is Unreal
We check further and see that there is no reality
to *'things'* apart from *Pure Existence (Brahman)*.
*'Thing'* is only a *name* given to a specific *form* and
*use* of *Existence*.
(Brahman did not cause the Universe and
*'things'* are only an *appearance* in *Brahman.*
Things don't exist. *Existence appears as things*.
We are not conscious of *'things'*. Things *appear* in
*Consciousness*.
The Universe *"appears"* in Brahman)

## Step 4: The Cause Loses Its Causality
The *Universe* or *'things'* are unreal therefore
*Brahman* cannot be called a *cause.*
*Brahman* remains as the Absolute Reality.
(Brahman loses its causality)

*"Today has been a long class but an important one. This will set the foundation for the next classes. All the examples talk about the same one reality in different ways and if you understand one of them, it becomes easier to understand the rest of them because the principles remain the same. I will see you tomorrow. We'll cover the Gold and Ornament example,"* said Dineshji as he walked out of the class.

*"He didn't even say a goodbye, how rude,"* said Eloa. *"Don't worry about him, follow me and let me take you to a place you'll remember for the rest of your lives,"* said Suraj, as they jumped onto their bikes and followed him. They cycled through small lanes and through the suburban alleys of Rishikesh for over three miles.

He led them to a place called *Chaurasi Kutia (84 huts).* They got off their bikes and walked towards a gate where they paid an entry fee of five hundred rupees per person and went in. *"This is the Beatles Ashram in Rishikesh,"* said Suraj as they walked towards some old buildings in ruins. *"You mean THE BEATLES???"* Exclaimed Asher and Eloa."

*"Yes the Beatles,"* replied Suraj. *"They came to India to learn Transcendental Meditation from a Guru by the name of Maharishi Mahesh Yogi in 1968. They spent many weeks at this ashram learning TM but also composed over forty of their greatest hit songs that featured on 'Abbey Road' and 'The White Album',"* said Suraj as they walked around the ruins that had graffiti paintings of the band members and sign boards reading what each building was used for.

Nelson, Asher and Eloa spent a good thirty minutes taking photos on their phone. It was the best place for them to visit as musicians. *"I wonder why the Beatles visited this place?"* asked Eloa. *"Let's ask one of the caretakers,"* replied Suraj walking towards a man in uniform and asked him in Hindi.

*"Well he said that the Beatles claimed that they had all the wealth and fame that they could ever ask for but it still didn't give them the peace and love that they were looking for. They met Maharishi Mahesh Yogi in Wales and decided to come and stay at the ashram to learn Transcendental Meditation from him."*

*"After their visit many foreigners, including celebrities flocked to Rishikesh to learn meditation and yoga. Since then Rishikesh has been a huge tourist destination,"* said Suraj. They walked out of the ashram and cycled home to a lovely homemade dinner and a short chitchat on the terrace. *"I wonder what Dineshji will talk about tomorrow,"* said Nelson, as they fell asleep.

# GOLD AND ORNAMENT

"*Good morning everyone,*" said Dineshji as everyone walked in and took their seats. "*Today we'll cover the Gold and Ornament example. It's very similar to the clay and pot example but because we covered that in depth yesterday, today's example won't take that long. In fact we should be able to breeze through it before lunch time.*"

"*Let's get started,*" said Dineshji as he got up and drew some ornaments on the blackboard. He drew a bangle, necklace, ring, earring and a pendant. At the top he wrote the words, "Gold And Ornaments".

"From yesterday's class, we came to know of a few universal truths that apply to everything in the Universe. We learnt that the Universe is made of 'things'. 'Things' are effects that have a cause. All things have a name, form and use. Names, forms and uses are not 'real' things in themselves; they depend on the existence of the cause. Without the 'cause' the thing cannot exist."

"Now, on the blackboard I have drawn a few ornaments that we all know of. There is a bangle, necklace, ring, earring and pendant. We'll assume that they're all made of Gold. If we look at them we see many 'things' made of gold but the material cause of all of them is gold."

"The things are many but the cause is one. Things are only names, forms and uses. So, the bangle, necklace, ring, earring and pendant all have different shapes, sizes and forms. They all have different names and they all have different uses. Every particle of each of the ornaments is made of gold. The ornaments are nothing apart from gold. The bangle, necklace, ring, earring and pendant cannot exist without gold but the gold can exist without the bangle, necklace, pendant and so on."

"The names, forms and uses are simply 'appearances' in gold. Gold alone is appearing as a bangle or necklace. If we smelt the ornaments, the names, forms and uses will disappear. The bangle will no longer be a bangle but the smelted gold will still be gold."

*"The shape, size and form of the bangle are nothing but the shape, size and form of the gold. The weight of the bangle is nothing but the weight of the gold. The value of the bangle is nothing but the value of the gold. When the bangle is smelted, the 'bangle' vanishes but the gold remains."*

*"What you see as a bangle is in fact gold. What you touch as the bangle is in fact gold. The 'thing' called 'bangle' is illusory. It is gold 'appearing' in a particular form and use. Always remember; what is 'real' does not 'appear' and what 'appears' is not real."*

*"In this case, gold 'appears' as a 'bangle'. Without the name (bangle) it is still gold, without the form (circular) it is still gold and without the use (to wear on the arm) it is still gold. BUT without the gold, there is no bangle."*

*"When you look at your face in the mirror your face 'appears' in the mirror looking exactly like your real face BUT it is not your real face. You cannot touch the face in the mirror; you cannot do anything to the face in the mirror. In the same way what we call a 'bangle' or 'necklace' looks exactly like gold in that particular form BUT it is not the gold. Gold is the reality and bangle is the appearance."*

*"Any questions so far?"* asked Dineshji looking at everyone. *"Acharyaji, comparing this to yesterday's example, gold is equivalent to clay and bangle is equivalent to pot. Gold and Clay are real but the different ornaments (of gold) and different objects (of clay) are only different forms of the same reality with different names and uses. I think that is correct,"* said Asher looking at Dineshji for confirmation.

*"That is correct,"* replied Dineshji, *"Let's see how the example relates with Brahman. Eloa I want you to imagine that you are this beautiful necklace made of gold,"* said Dineshji. *"Okay,"* replied Eloa cheerfully.

*"Eloa, you feel, think and know yourself to be a necklace. In fact everything you do is done as a necklace. Now tell me, what else do you see in the Universe of Gold?"* asked Dineshji looking at Eloa.

*"On the blackboard I see a ring, a bangle, an earring and a pendant but if I use my imagination, everything good or bad including the garbage is made of gold,"* replied Eloa. *"Can you be destroyed?"* asked Dineshji. *"Yes, being a necklace I can be destroyed,"* replied Eloa. *"In your Universe can gold be destroyed?"* asked Dineshji.

"*Nope! Gold cannot be destroyed. The ornament can be destroyed but gold remains as it is!*" Exclaimed Eloa looking excited. "*That's a wonderful answer Eloa,*" said Dineshji.

"*In the same way Brahman (Pure Existence and Consciousness) cannot be destroyed. Things can be destroyed but Brahman (Pure Existence and Consciousness) remains as it is!*" Exclaimed Dineshji. "*Good for Brahman Acharyaji, what about us, we will all die someday,*" said Suraj from where he was seated.

"*You are Brahman! You were never born and cannot die! The pot will die, not clay! The necklace will die, not gold! The body will die, not Brahman! The pot has to realize itself as clay. The necklace has to realize itself as gold and you have to realize yourself as Brahman (Pure Existence and Consciousness),*" replied Dineshji looking at Suraj.

"*Nelson can you write the four steps that I explained yesterday on the blackboard please. Replace clay with gold,*" asked Dineshji handing him the piece of chalk. "*Sure Acharyaji,* replied Nelson as he got up and wrote on the blackboard.

## Step 1: The Thing or Effect
We start with a *'thing'* or *'effect'* called *'Bangle'*.
(Bangle = Effect)

## Step 2: The Cause Of The Effect
The cause is always found in the effect.
We check the *'Bangle'* for its cause.
The *Bangle* is made of one reality called *'Gold'*.
(Gold = Cause, Bangle = Effect)

## Step 3: The 'Thing' Or 'Effect' Is Unreal
We check further and see that there is no such
'thing' as a 'Bangle'. 'Bangle' is only a *name* given
to a specific *form* and *use* of *Gold*.
(Gold did not cause any new *'thing'* and
*'Bangle'* is only an *appearance* of *Gold*)

## Step 4: The Cause Loses Its Causality
The *effect* is unreal therefore Gold cannot be
called a *cause.* Only Gold remains as the reality.
(Gold loses its causality)

*"That is awesome and absolutely correct,
I'll see you tomorrow when we'll cover the Wave
and Ocean example,"* said Dineshji as he walked
out of the class. *"Why does he just walk out of the
class once he's done,"* asked Asher to the rest of
them as they came out and got on to their bikes.
They had more than half the day to explore
Rishikesh...

*"This is great. We have enough time to go for some real adventure,"* said Suraj as they rode out of Achintya Village towards *Laxman Jhula* and parked their bikes outside the local police station. *"Where are we going?"* asked Nelson as they followed Suraj. He hurried towards a small office that had a signboard reading *'Jumpin Heights'.* They all waited outside as Suraj returned with four tickets.

*"This minibus will take us to Jumpin Heights"* said Suraj excitedly. *"You're all going to love this place. It's one of its kind in India and Asia,"* said Suraj, as the bus started moving. *"It will take about forty minutes to get there. I can't wait,"* said Suraj looking even more excited now.

*"What is Jumpin Heights?"* asked Eloa and Nelson. Asher pulled out some leaflets that were placed in the seat pockets in front of them. Eloa, Nelson and Asher went through the leaflet, *"Bungee Jumping!!!!! Yay! I've always wanted to do that. This is awesome!"* Exclaimed Eloa looking excited herself now.

*"Seriously? Bungee jumping in India?"* asked Asher looking a little nervous. *"Not only that, they have India's most extreme Giant Swing and Asia's longest Flying Fox!"* Exclaimed Suraj and everyone checked the leaflet to know more about what that was.

The little mini bus had about twelve passengers including the four of them. When they reached the place, it was was packed with tourists and they had to stand in line for their tickets and turn to come. The bungee jumping is at a height of eighty-three meters with professional trainers from New Zealand. Standing on the platform before jumping they could see the entire valley below them and a small tributary of the Ganges River.

They all gathered the courage to make the jump one by one. They had paid for all three activities as a combo deal. After the jump, it was a twenty-minute walk back up to the same platform for the *Giant Swing*. The *Giant Swing* was very similar to the bungee jump except that the person was strapped in a sitting position and after the fall, the person swung like a pendulum before coming to rest.

Finally they went for the *Flying Fox* where they were harnessed in a lying facing down position and released from the platform. They rolled down a cable at a speed of 160Kmph up to just a few meters above the river. It was an amazing and exciting experience.

After the rides, they sat in the cafeteria waiting for their videos and pictures of the rides. *"This is truly an amazing place to visit,"* said Asher as they sat in the minibus that took them back to *Laxman Jhula*. They picked their bikes and headed back home exhausted and hungry, but looking forward to tomorrow's class.

# WAVE AND OCEAN

The next morning in the classroom Dineshji started with his lesson. *"Today we'll cover the Wave and Ocean example. In this example we have a single wave on the surface of the ocean among millions of other waves. The wave has the same problem as the pot and the necklace in that it thinks and knows itself to be a wave that will surely be destroyed someday."*

*"The Ocean is the Universe for the wave and all the other millions of waves. Let's call our little wave Mr. Wave. So, Mr. Wave sees all types of waves in his Universe. Big waves, small waves, fast waves, slow waves, happy waves, sad waves and so on. They all know for sure that when they hit the shore they're going to die."*

*"Now, we'll examine the thing called a 'wave' in the same manner that we examined the 'pot' and 'bangle' to find out the Absolute Reality of the entity called a wave. To begin with we have a single wave. Due to the law of cause and effect, we can easily examine to determine the material cause of the thing called a wave."*

*"If we look at the wave, we can clearly see that it is made up of Water. Now we have a wave that is made of something called 'water'. If we look more closely at the wave we realize that the wave is entirely made up of water. It is water from the inside, outside, up and down. There is no other thing apart from water in the wave."*

*"So if the entire wave is water, then what or where is the wave? Upon further investigation we realize that 'wave' is only a name given to a particular form of water with a particular use or function. Just like the pot and the bangle, the wave too is only an 'appearance' of its cause."*

*"Thus the wave is not real but an appearance of water in a particular form. We realize that the wave is illusory and water is its reality. When the wave learns about water, it realizes that the entire Ocean is nothing but water. After the wave gets enlightened and identifies itself as water, it realizes that the wave, the millions of other waves and the ocean are all appearances in itself (water)."*

*"I've just gone over this quickly because the same principles that we used for the clay and pot example, and gold and ornament examples apply. Understanding any one of them clearly makes it very easy to understand the other two."*

*"Let's take a look at how this example relates to you, the Universe and Brahman. Water is equivalent to Brahman. The wave is equivalent to you and the Ocean is equivalent to the Universe."*

*"The wave is going through a wave life just like you are going through your life. The wave feels separate from the rest of the waves around it and the entire ocean just as you feel separate from everything around you and the entire Universe. The wave has never heard of water just as you have never heard of Brahman."*

*"The smallest molecule of water is made up of two atoms of hydrogen and one atom of oxygen i.e. $H_2O$. One molecule of $H_2O$ is water. A billion molecules of $H_2O$ put together is still water. This molecule is too small to be seen by the naked eye."*

*"When the wave learns of water and examines itself, it realizes that it is entirely made up of water. It also fails to find a real thing called a wave. It looks out at the other waves and realizes they are all nothing but water."*

*"When its false identity is replaced by the true identity as water, the wave becomes one with the entire Ocean. In fact the Ocean and millions of waves, all 'appear' in water. We can also say that water alone is appearing as the Ocean and waves."*

*"In the same way when you learn about Brahman and examine yourself, you will realize that every bit to your body and mind is made up of Brahman (Pure Existence and Consciousness). If you investigate further, you will fail to find what or where the ego is because it is unreal. The ego is just an, 'I' thought in the mind and your thoughts also 'appear' in Brahman. If you look at everything and everybody in the Universe, you will realize that they all 'appear' in Brahman (Pure Existence and Consciousness) too."*

*"When your false ego is replaced by your true identity as Brahman, you become one with the entire Universe. In fact the Universe and millions of things all 'appear' in you as Brahman. Let's take a look at the four steps of the law of cause and effect using water. Asher, would you write it out for us on the blackboard please? I just want to make sure you've all understood the examples well enough,"* said Dineshji handing the chalk to Asher. Asher went to the blackboard and wrote the following.

## Step 1: The Thing or Effect
We start with a *'thing'* or *'effect'* called *'Wave'*.
(Wave = Effect)

## Step 2: The Cause Of The Effect
The cause is always found in the effect.
We check the *'Wave'* for its cause.
The *Wave* is made of one reality called *'Water'*.
(Water = Cause, Wave = Effect)

## Step 3: The 'Thing' Or 'Effect' Is Unreal
We check further and see that there is no such
'thing' as a 'Wave'. 'Wave' is only a *name* given to
a specific *form* and *use* of *Water*.
(Water did not cause any new *'thing'* and
*'Wave'* is only an *appearance* of *Water*)

## Step 4: The Cause Loses Its Causality
The *effect* is unreal therefore Water cannot be
called a *cause*. Only Water remains as the reality.
(Water loses its causality)

*"Great job Asher. Can you repeat the same
example with regard to our Universe and
Brahman like I did on the first day just as a
revision exercise?"* said Dineshji. Asher proceeded
to write on the empty part of the blackboard.

## Step 1: The Thing or Effect
We start with a *'thing'* or *'effect'* called *'Universe'*.
(Universe = Effect)

## Step 2: The Cause Of The Effect
The cause is always found in the effect.
We check the *'Universe'* for its cause.
The Universe is made *'things'* that *EXIST*.
We check *'things'* for their *cause*
*'Things'* or the *Universe* is made of one reality
called *Existence*. Things that *'exist'* make the
Universe. Without *Existence* itself there can be no
*thing* or *Universe.*
(Brahman = Cause, Universe = Effect)

## Step 3: The 'Thing' Or 'Effect' Is Unreal
We check further and see that there is no reality
to *'things'* apart from *Pure Existence (Brahman)*.
*'Thing'* is only a *name* given to a specific *form* and
*use* of *Existence.*
(Brahman did not cause the Universe and
*'things'* are only an *appearance* in *Brahman.*
Things don't exist. *Existence appears as things.*
We are not conscious of *'things'*. Things *appear* in
*Consciousness.*
The Universe *"appears"* in Brahman)

## Step 4: The Cause Loses Its Causality
The *Universe* or *'things'* are unreal therefore
*Brahman* cannot be called a *cause.*
*Brahman* remains as the Absolute Reality.
(Brahman loses its causality)

Dineshji looked very pleased with his students. *"Thank you Asher. We are done with the main three examples used in Vedanta to explain how you are not what you think or know yourself to be, and that your true identity is Brahman in which the entire Universe including your body and mind 'appear'. I'll draw a table to conclude these three examples for your easy reference."*

*"For the next three days the examples we will discuss are about how and why we see everything in the Universe as it is instead of seeing Brahman everywhere. We'll try to understand why we only perceive the 'appearance' instead of the reality of the Universe,"* said Dineshji as he walked out of the classroom leaving the rest wondering if the lesson was over or he would be coming back.

| Individual Thing | Individual's Universe | The Universe's Reality | The Reality's Inherent Power |
|---|---|---|---|
| Pot | Ceramics & Pottery | Clay | Cohesion Of Clay Particles |
| Necklace | Gold Ornaments & Objects | Gold | Cohesion Of Gold Atoms |
| Wave | Ocean With Millions Of Waves | Water | Cohesion Of Water Molecules |
| You | Universe Of Millions Of Things | Brahman (Pure Existence and Pure Consciousness) | Maya (Cohesion Of Existence & Consciousness) |

**Cohesion** is the action or fact of forming a united whole. It is the **power** of sticking together of particles of the **same substance**.

Clay particles, Gold atoms and Water molecules stick together due to cohesion, which allow shapes and forms to be projected.

In the same way, all *things* are stuck together in *Existence* and *Consciousness*. *Maya* projects *Existence* and *Consciousness* to appear as separate *things* in the Universe. All *things* are stuck together in and by *Existence* and *Consciousness* to form one united whole Universe.

# APPEARANCE VERSUS REALITY EXAMPLES

It was the fourth day and they were all seated in the class. *"Today I'm going to share some small examples that are widely used in Vedanta to illustrate why things 'appear' to be what they're not. Remember in the past three days we discussed how clay 'appears' to be a pot, how gold 'appears' to be a bangle and how water 'appears' to be a wave,"* said Dineshji.

*"Whenever we say that something 'appears' to be xyz, we mean that it is NOT xyz but is something else. This something else is the material cause or reality of the xyz. When we said water 'appears' as a wave, we mean that what we see in NOT a wave, it's reality is something else."*

## Snake In The Rope:

"We'll start with the Snake in the Rope example. Imagine that you're walking down a small alleyway in the night with only the moonlight shining. In the distance, a few feet away from you, you notice something like a snake lying on the ground. You would immediately stop, get terrified or at least become alert and aware of it."

"The fear of getting bitten by a snake will make you extra cautious. The snake is obstructing your path and you need to go through the alleyway to reach your home. You look around and find a metal rod lying on the side. Picking it up you cautiously walk towards where the snake is lying and as you come near it, before it pounces on you, you hit it hard on its body with the rod."

"As it moves, you hit it a few more times. When you stop to see whether its still alive, it seems to be dead, not moving or breathing at all. You walk slowly up to it and pin it down with the rod once more looking for where its head is. When you find one of its ends and pick it up, you realize it's not a snake but a rope that looked like a snake."

"Your first reaction is to breathe a sigh of relief realizing that it isn't a poisonous snake like you thought all along. It's a harmless piece of rope. The fear disappeared with the knowledge of the rope. Until then you were ignorant of the rope and feared what you saw."

*"Because you didn't know it was a rope you immediately assumed that it was a snake and that 'error' led to fear, caution and everything that followed. The snake was 'superimposed' on the rope. Every bit of the rope 'looked' like a snake because of ignorance. Once knowledge is gained and the truth is known, the rope may still look like a snake from a distance, but it won't frighten you anymore."*

*"In the same way, the entire Universe is superimposed on you. Because you don't know your true identity as Brahman, you immediately assumed that you are a person with a body-mind complex. This 'error' leads to everything 'you' (mistaken identity) experience in life. It gives rise to fear, jealousy, competition, sadness, happiness, death, pain, suffering and all the ups and downs of life."*

*"The error of mistaken identity limits you to your body and mind. And this little person sees a Universe outside him or her. Everything in the Universe 'appears' to be separate from you. The world of opposites and duality comes into play. The body was born and will die, you feel happy and sadness, you experience the ups and downs of life. Life throws everything at you and you go through it having no option."*

*"All this because you have wrongly identified yourself as the body-mind complex. Vedanta says when you realize the truth about yourself and the Universe; you will breathe the sigh of relief just like when you realized the snake was a harmless rope."*

*"Your true Self is Brahman (Pure Existence and Consciousness) which means that the entire Universe is nothing but you. If you realize your true Self as Brahman, then what is it that you would fear? What would you desire? Who is there to compete with? What would you be worried about? You would transcend every 'thing' in the Universe."*

*"The body-mind complex would still carry on with life till the body dies but you as Brahman are never born and can never die. I have explained this example in detail and depth because the next few examples are very similar and we'll be able to go over them quickly having understood this one clearly. Any questions?"* asked Dineshji looking at everyone.

*"Is there a Universe of ropes that we have to assume in this example like we did in the earlier ones?"* asked Nelson. *"No! These examples are about how and why one thing 'appears' to be what it is not. So we need 'you' to observe the 'thing' in the example. It is from your point of view and not the rope's point of view,"* replied Dineshji. *"Then it's quite straight forward and clear,"* said Nelson.

## Ghost In The Post

*"This is very similar to the 'Snake in the Rope' example. Imagine you are walking through the woods under the dim moonlight and you suddenly see a black ghostly figure with weird arms spread open as through it were charging towards you,"* said Dineshji.

*"You would immediately get frightened and scared just as you did with the snake. Fear would set in and many thoughts and actions would follow because of what you saw. Finally when you realize that the figure hasn't moved from where it was, you gather the courage to go closer to investigate."*

*"It turns out to be a dead tree stump with two dry branches to its sides that makes it appear as a scary ghost under the dim moonlight. You breathe a sigh of relief on realizing it to be a harmless dead tree stump."*

*"The ghost was superimposed on the post. It 'appeared' to be a scary ghost due to ignorance. When ignorance is removed by knowledge the truth is revealed and you are at ease. In the same way when you realize that the Universe isn't what it 'appears' to be but is superimposed on you (Brahman) everything is transcended and you are eternally at ease. Any questions?"* asked Dineshji.
*"No,"* came the unanimous reply.

## Desert And Mirage

*"In this example a man is seen walking through the desert. After a few days, he has run out of his food and water supply. Under the blazing sun he walks looking for something to quench his thirst. In the distance he sees what seems to be a large Oasis full of water,"* said Dineshji.

*"He hurries towards it and as he gets closer, he realizes the oasis has moved further ahead. He hurries to that spot only to find that there is no water there but he sees another oasis in the distance. He struggles to get there only to find that there's no water."*

*"He keeps wandering in the desert wondering how and why the water in the oasis kept moving away from him. Whenever he got to the spot where he would be able to quench his thirst, he realizes that there is no water yet it clearly looked like water from a distance."*

*"He may keep wandering in the desert until he realizes that the water in the oasis is not real but an illusion created by the sun's rays on the hot sand. The sand 'appears' as water from a distance. When the man learns of this illusion known as a mirage, he stops wandering about aimlessly after every mirage he sees in the desert and sticks to his journey."*

*"In the same way there are many mirages in our lives that we see everyday and work towards hoping that they will give us happiness and peace. We find many things and people in whom we try to find happiness and we keep doing it for years and years. Only the wise will understand that nothing and nobody can give him the everlasting love, peace, joy and happiness that he has been seeking for decades."*

*"Eternal peace, happiness, love and joy are not found in things or people. It can only be gotten when you realize your true Self, that is bliss itself, peace itself, love itself and joy itself. Once you realize your true Self as Brahman, you are not happy but happiness itself, you are not peaceful but peace itself, you are not in love but love itself and so on."*

*"The mistaken identity leads us to believe that external things and people can give us joy and happiness. The wise realize soon that none of it is permanent and there is no end to it. There is always a new gadget that you want, the latest car, a bigger house, a world tour etc. They appear to give you happiness and joy."*

*"In reality your true Self is pure bliss itself and here you are running after little illusory joys and sense pleasures. Nothing in the Universe can make you happy because your true nature is happiness itself."*

# Vedanta Examples Simplified

# UNTOUCHED BRAHMAN EXAMPLES

*"Now we will look at three examples that describe how Brahman is unaffected and untouched by the Universe. These are very similar to understanding how the clay is unaffected if the pot breaks or how the gold is unaffected if the bangle is melted and formed into a pair or earrings."*

*"The clay is untouched by the pot, the gold is untouched by the bangle, the water is untouched by the wave and you as Brahman are untouched by the Universe,"* said Dineshji.

## Lotus Leaf And Water

*"Your true identity as Brahman is completely untouched by everything going on in your life and the Universe. It transcends everything including pain and suffering, birth and death. When you realize yourself as Brahman, you realize that you are unborn and immortal. You also realize that you are merely a witness to everything happening in your life and the Universe. A witness who is unaffected, untouched and unchanged in any way by what is going on."*

*"In this example we have a Lotus leaf in a pond or lake. The lotus leaf has a special quality that doesn't allow water to wet the leaf. When water falls on the leaf it remains as little drops of water completely unattached to the leaf. The water drops simply roll off the leaf without a trace of its presence."*

*"In the same way, your true Self, Brahman, is completely untouched by the ups and downs of life including birth and death. Brahman stays as it is eternally. The water on the Lotus leaf appears and disappears but the Lotus leaf stays as it is, unaffected and untouched. The Universe appears and disappears but you as Brahman stay as you are, unaffected and untouched,"* said Dineshji.

## Air And Scent

"This example is similar to the previous one. Wind carries whatever scent is exposed to it and spreads it everywhere. The scents can be pleasant or unpleasant but the air, in which they spread, is always pure. The air is untouched and never gets affected by the scents that arise and subside in it."

"In the same way everything in the Universe arises and subsides in Brahman but Brahman remains pure always. Brahman is not tainted, stained or affected in any way. You as Brahman remain pure and untouched by the arising and subsiding Universe."

## Space And Jar

"In this example we have a jar that has space in it. We know that space is one of the five elements that the Universe is made of, the other four being fire, air, water and earth. Of all these, space is the most pervasive. All four elements appear or exist in space. So, the entire Universe is in space or we can say that Space pervades the entire Universe. There is nowhere that Space is not!"

"Now, the jar has space inside it which is used to store different items. We can say that the space in the jar is different from the space outside the jar. Once the lid is on, we assume the space inside to be isolated from the space outside."

"However, the space only 'appears' to be divided. In reality, space is completely untouched by the existence of the jar. There is no inside or outside as far as space is concerned. Space simply is! The jar may appear to divide the space but in reality the space is untouched and unaffected by the jar. When you move the jar from one position to another, it appears that the space in the jar is also moving with the jar, but in reality it is the jar that is moving through space. Space remains untouched, unaffected and unstained."

"A wall in a room creates the illusion of dividing space in the room. In reality space is unaffected. In the same way you as Brahman are all pervading and completely untouched and unaffected by everything going on in the Universe," said Dineshji looking at everyone if they were following.

"That's all for today," said Dineshji, "Tomorrow we'll look at some examples that explain what is seen from the enlightened person's point of view," said Dineshji as he hurried out of the class. "He's gone again. Does no one say a goodbye in this place?" asked Eloa looking at Suraj.

*"Forget that, today we'll go river-rafting and cliff jumping. It will be really exciting,"* said Suraj as they followed him on their bikes. They opted for mildest river rafting from *Brahmapuri to Rishikesh*, which is a 9km long stretch on the Ganges River. It was the easiest and mildest river-rafting route for beginners. They put on the life jackets provided and joined two other couples on the raft.

*"I thought they said this would be mild,"* screamed Eloa as they sped down the river with water splashing on them and the raft almost overturning a number of times. They covered the 9km in one and a half hours.

*"That was awesome,"* said Asher as they stepped out of the raft. *"Rishikesh has some amazing places Suraj. I thought it would be boring but I must say that I'm really surprised and glad that we came here,"* said Eloa holding Nelson's hand as they walked.

They headed to the cliff-jumping place in the *Shivalik* region of Rishikesh. A place that has cliffs of varied heights embraced by the holy Ganges River. Jumping from a height of twenty feet into the river was another thrilling and adventurous experience for all of them.

Fully wet, they decided to sit by the cliff for some time as they watched other people jump into the river. Some jumped from around ten feet while others went as high as thirty feet.

After sometime they rode all the way home. Although everyone was tired and exhausted they all wanted to explore more. *"Tonight we'll go cafe hopping. Just like in California everyone goes club hopping, in Rishikesh everyone goes cafe hopping,"* said Suraj once they were home. Everyone showered and freshened up putting on a clean pair of clothes and all ready for the night.

*"We'll start with 'The 60's Cafe', which is very popular for its good music, good vibes, good food and breathtaking view of the Ram Jhula Bridge over the Ganges River,"* said Suraj as they walked out the bungalow. *"It's a twenty minute walk from here,"* said Suraj as they set out on foot through the city and shops that were still buzzing with activity.

*Rock n roll* tunes from the 60's played at the cafe and the menu comprised of a variety of vegan, gluten free and green juices in cuisines from all over the world. A table facing the spiritual *Ram Jhula Bridge*, great food and music with awesome service was the most memorable time spent that evening.

The other cafes that they hopped to included *Bistro Nirvana* and *Ellbee Ganga View*, which had their own specialties. They got back home way past midnight. *"What an awesome place this is. I'm in love with Rishikesh. Please wake me up early,"* said Asher as they walked off into their rooms.

# THE ENLIGHTENED PERSON
# EXAMPLES

Next morning at Achintya Village, *"Today we'll look at six short examples that are used to describe the enlightened person (knower of Brahman) and two others that describe how we should pursue the realization of Brahman,"* said Dineshji.

*"They are very short and simple examples which I'm sure you will have no difficulty understanding straightaway. So let's begin,"* said Dineshji.

## Burnt Cloth

"In this example when a piece of cloth is burnt completely you will see that after the fire has completely diffused, the piece of cloth will have retained its form. However, when you touch it with your hand even slightly it is reduced to ashes immediately. The form only appears but has no reality or substance to it."

"In the same way the enlightened person's body only appears to exist but has no reality to it. His body is like the burnt cloth retaining a form of a person that has no reality to it. No reality means there is no ego trying to sustain it."

## Butter In Milk

"This example is used to explain how Brahman is the reality of the Universe even though it cannot be perceived in any way. Butter and ghee (clarified butter) exists in milk. Yet you cannot see or perceive butter in milk in any way. Butter is present in every drop of milk but we can't see it. In the same way, you as Brahman pervade the entire Universe but cannot be perceived."

"Just because we can't see the butter in milk doesn't mean it is not there. It is present in every drop. In the same way just because we can't perceive Brahman anywhere doesn't mean it's not there. It is there in every thing. However, the man who churns milk to make butter knows that butter pervades milk. In the same way the knower of Brahman (enlightened person) knows Brahman pervades the Universe."

## Fire In Wood

"This is very similar to the previous example of Butter in Milk. Fire is present in all parts of wood. Any and every part of wood has fire present in it. We can't see the fire but that doesn't mean its not there. We can see the fire when it manifests as visible flames. Fire pervades wood in the un-manifested state but we only pay attention to it in the manifested state."

"However, the man who collects firewood knows that fire pervades the wood. In the same way the knower of Brahman (enlightened person) knows Brahman pervades the Universe."

## Two Birds In A Tree

"In this example we have two identical birds who live in the same tree. One bird is very busy in eating the fruits, building its nest, laying eggs, looking after its chicks and constantly jumping from one branch to another. It is completely engrossed, bound and attached to all its activities in the tree. The second bird sits at the treetop looking down at the first bird. It doesn't do anything at all. It simply remains as a witness to what the first bird is doing."

"In the same way it is said that the person and the Absolute Reality Brahman reside in the same body. The person remains ever busy with the Universe while the Absolute Reality Brahman remains as a witness to all the activities of the person without ever interfering or getting affected. The enlightened person abides as Brahman witnessing the person going through life without ever getting involved or getting affected by what the person is doing. He is free of the person and simply witnesses his or her activities."

## Two Thorns

*"In this example imagine you are walking through the forest and step on some thorns and one thorn gets stuck in your foot. The best and easiest way to remove the thorn at the time would be to take another thorn and remove the one stuck in the foot. Once it is removed, you should throw away both the thorns. The second thorn was used to remove the first one, and having done so, there is no reason to keep any of them."*

*"In the same way, we need to realize our true Self. We are stuck in doing; saying and thinking everything we can to get spiritually enlightened. We are stuck in ignorance of our true identity. The best way to get out of this is to use the second thorn of doing, saying and thinking through spiritual practices including Selfless work, Meditation, Love, Devotion and Knowledge to attain spiritual enlightenment."*

*"Having attained Spiritual enlightenment we should cast off both ignorance and knowledge, both unenlightened and enlightened states and simply abide as our true Self. Take the thorn of knowledge and remove the thorn of ignorance, then discard them both. None of the spiritual practices used to help realize the Self are useful after realization and should be discarded,"* said Dineshji.

## The Chameleon

*"The Chameleon is the only animal that can and does change its color to match the color of the surface it is moving on. This helps it to remain camouflaged which is absolutely necessary for its survival given that it is also one of the slowest moving animals on the planet."*

*"In the example we have a person who has seen the chameleon in red color and hence he thinks it is red in color. Another person has seen it while it was green and he assumes that the chameleon is a green animal. But the person who has watched the chameleon closely as it keeps changing its color know the truth."*

*"Vedanta says it is dangerous to have only partial knowledge of anything. This leads to quarrels among people. Some people say God is like this and other say He is like that but only the person who understands the whole existence knows the true nature of the Universe and God. He has no doubts about himself, the Universe or God. He or she knows them all to be the same one Absolute Reality – Brahman,"* said Dineshji.

*"Now the next two examples are very simple and they describe how one should attain the knowledge of Brahman. Let's see what they have to say,"* said Dineshji.

## Arundhati Star

*"The Arundhati Star is a considered as sacred in the Hindu culture. It is unique because it consists of two stars close to one another that revolve around in a circle. The stars are very faintly visible and in one of the rituals of the Hindu marriage, the groom has to show the bride the double stars as a symbol of marital fulfillment and loyalty. But because of the faint visibility, the double stars have to be shown gradually in steps. If one points out directly to the star the person will definitely not be able to see it."*

*"So the husband takes his wife step by step and points out to a treetop, then points out a bigger brighter star just above the treetop, then leads her to see a few smaller stars finally coming to the very faintly visible Arundhati Star. This example is used to illustrate that the seeker of the truth has to be taken step by step from where he or she is to the truth."*

*"So the seeker of spiritual enlightenment cannot simply be told, 'That Thou Art' and expect him or her to realize his or her true Self right away. They have to be guided gradually to the direct realization of Brahman. The steps may be any or all the spiritual practices prescribed by various scriptures,"* said Dineshji.

## Monkey And Its Baby

*"The monkey and its baby have a very special bonding. From the baby's point of view, it is completely attached to the mother. It grabs hold of its mother's chest and never leaves it even in times of extreme danger. At times, even when the mother is dead you may find the baby still holding on to her chest. No matter what the calamity or danger, it doesn't let go."*

*"This example is used to illustrate what the nature of a seeker of should be like. He or she does not rely on any external help or grace for their salvation or freedom. They grab hold onto their chosen path and don't let go no matter what comes their way until they realize their true Brahman - Self,"* said Dineshji.

*"These are the most common examples that are used to explain what Brahman is 'like', not what it is but what it is like. Does anyone have any questions regarding any of the examples that we discussed over the week?"* asked Dineshji.

*"Not really Acharyaji, I think you have been very clear in the way you presented the logic and theories. I agree with everything that you've said. I have no problems with any of the examples you taught us. And I also understand what I'm about to ask you cannot be explained in any way,"* said Nelson.

*"Please ask Nelson. Brighter minds than yours and mine have questioned the Vedanta philosophy and received satisfactory answers. So don't be shy, please ask,"* said Dineshji.

*"Acharyaji, I know Brahman is not a thing or an object and all the examples you taught us involved different things and the reality from their point of view. But from our point of view since Brahman is not a thing, we can't know it, see it, hear it, smell it, taste it, touch it imagine it, dream it or do anything to or with it."*

*"You also mentioned that Brahman is Pure Existence. We all know that things exist because we can perceive them with our senses and mind but Pure Existence is not a thing so we can't perceive it with our senses or mind. You also said that Brahman is Pure Consciousness. We all know that we are conscious or aware but Pure Consciousness is not a thing that can be perceived with our senses or mind. Yet we can't deny the fact that if things exist, then there must be 'existence' being perceived along with the things. We also can't deny the fact that if we are conscious of things, then there must be 'consciousness'."*

*"I agree with all that but a doubt arises whether Pure Existence or Pure Consciousness is possible. Is it possible to perceive everything as existence and perceive it all in consciousness? It would be like the Universe perceiving itself. Is that a possibility and that too when you say I am Brahman, it means I am the Universe perceiving itself. It sounds profound but doubtful,"* said Nelson looking at Dineshji.

*"Wow! You are certainly an A-grade student Nelson. Everything that you have just said is absolutely correct. You have completed two of the three steps in Vedanta, which are Shravanam and Mananam. Shravanam means listening to the scriptures and knowing what they say. Not necessarily understand or agree with what they're saying but being able to repeat what they said."*

*"The second step is Mananam which means understanding what the scriptures are saying. This comes after clearing all possible doubts that arise in the mind. Having understood the scriptures you can confidently say, 'I know what the scriptures say and now I get it'. From what you have just shared, it seems that you have heard everything I said and have understood it beyond a doubt."*

*"The third step is Nidhidhyasana which means 'marinating' yourself or 'meditating' on what you have understood in every action in your life until it becomes a living reality for you. This step is not understanding intellectually but direct realization. This is Spiritual Enlightenment. I cannot teach you realization and in fact no one can, only you can realize your true Self as Brahman."*

*"It can take a lifetime to realize it or it could take a few months depending on how determined and sincerely you pursue it,"* said Dineshji looking very pleased with Nelson.

*"I guess you're right Acharyaji. This is an eye opener that is not taught in any schools or universities. It is something that I must realize having understood what it is like through the examples you explained. I have to realize myself as the entire 'Existence in Consciousness' while the drama of the Universe plays upon it,"* said Nelson shaking his head in disbelief.

Dineshji got up and came and gave Nelson a warm hug. *"You are the first student in my sixteen years of teaching, that I can honestly say I am proud of. Today, you have made me feel worthy of being called an Acharya,"* said Dineshji as he wiped off a tear that rolled down his cheeks. *"Suraj, give my regards to your father,"* he said as put his books into an old worn out bag and walked out of the classroom.

They all walked out feeling emotional as they got onto their bikes and rode out of Achintya Village stopping by the *Little Buddha Cafe* for a cup of coffee. *"How can we repay this man's kindness?"* asked Nelson as the waiter took their order.

*"He didn't charge us a penny, he's been wearing tattered clothes every single day. I bet he's been walking to the village and leaving on foot as well. He's going around different villages teaching what he knows for free and still no one cares or attends,"* said Nelson looking at the rest of them as tears dropped from his eyes.

*"Hey calm down Nelson,"* said Suraj, *"I've known Dinesh Uncle since childhood and he's always been a very honest man. Even though he is a close friend of my father and we are well off financially, he has never asked for any financial help as far as I can remember. Ramu, his son is quite young but could never attend school because Dinesh uncle couldn't afford it. Ramu's mother works at people's houses as a maid cleaning floors and washing utensils to earn some money,"* said Suraj.

*"What would be the school fees in a decent school here,"* asked Asher, *"Oh, you'll be surprised, compared to what we pay in USA this is peanuts. Only with the amount of money we spent on all the adventurous activities here, he would have attended school for a year,"* replied Suraj.

"*What!*" Exclaimed Eloa and Nelson. "*Look I think we should do something in return for them. I have about six hundred dollars that I can spare. I'm not sure how much that is in rupees,*" said Nelson "*That's a great idea. I too can spare about five hundred dollars,* " said Eloa. "*I have about two hundred dollars that I can spare,*" said Asher.

"*That's thirteen hundred dollars. What do you think Suraj,*" said Nelson looking at him. "*It's a huge amount of money. I can't add any money from my side because Dinesh uncle won't accept it but if he knows it's from his students, I'm sure he will have no objections. It's called 'Guru Dakshina', which is what a student offers back to his or her teacher as a gift after the learning is complete.*"

"*I'm sure Dad can organize admission for Ramu in a decent school locally and the amount you guys are willing to give will easily pay his school fees for the next three years. You guys are crazy and all I can say is Asante Sana. I'm sure Dinesh uncle and Ramu will both appreciate it a lot,*" said Suraj as they enjoyed their beverages overseeing the holy Ganges."

When they got home, Suraj narrated the plan they had to pay for Ramu's education as *Guru Dakshina* to Dinesh Acharyaji. He was well impressed with all four of them and promised to ensure Ramu got admission in one of the good schools around.

After dinner they all went up to the terrace to hang out. *"Well, Suraj I think we'll have to cancel the rest of our tour because none of us has any more money left,"* said Eloa sadly. *"Yes I thought so too but it's not the money issue, our return flight from Goa is in two days time. We have spent all our days in Rishikesh without realizing it,"* said Asher.

*"Don't worry guys. Tomorrow will be my treat. There are still a few must see places here that we can explore. We'll fly back to Goa on the day after tomorrow,"* said Suraj smiling.

The next day Suraj took them out for *kayaking, hot air ballooning, shopping, mountain biking, Ayurvedic massages and exploring some of the ancient temples* before they returned home late in the night, having had an awesome day.

The following morning they all had their bags packed, the taxi was outside waiting for them. They all bid Suraj's parents goodbye and as they were leaving, Dinesh Acharyaji and Ramu came to thank them. They both had tears in their eyes, *"Ramu, study well and I'm sure we'll be back soon to see how you're doing,"* said Nelson ruffling Ramu's hair with his hand.

The cab left and the *Asante Sana Band* flew to Goa just in time to catch their return flight to California.

# EXTRA NOTES

*"Hopefully you are not more confused but have understood the examples well enough to come up with your own examples using only the concept of appearance and reality. Let me give you a few examples. We all wear clothes that have different shapes, sizes, names, colors, styles and so on. The reality of every piece of cloth is 'thread'. Only thread is woven to appear as a shirt or a dress. Dress = appearance. Thread = reality."*

*"Plastic spoons, forks, buckets, cups, plates and every item made of plastic only differs in name, form and use of one reality called plastic. Spoon = appearance, Plastic = reality."*

All the examples urge us to realize the reality of what we're perceiving so that we realize the truth of whatever it is that we are perceiving. If you remember a few facts it will make it easier to analyze any Vedantic example.

**We are in a Universe.**
**Our Universe is made up of *THINGS*.**
**Every*THING* together is our Universe.**
**Every*THING* has a cause.**
**The cause is found in the *THING*.**
**The cause is *Real* and the *thing* is unreal.**
**Whatever *appears* is unreal.**
**Whatever is real *never* appears.**

Now from our point of view we can understand how clay is the reality in a clay Universe and how water is the reality of the Ocean and waves. This is because both the reality and the appearances are *objects in our understanding.*

The difficulty with Brahman is that every*THING* in our Universe is also unreal. Even the mind and intellect we are trying to use to realize or understand Brahman is unreal. We are trying to realize Brahman (which is not a thing) with our mind (which is a thing).

The mind is some*thing* and Brahman is no*thing.* Only when we remove all things including our bodies, minds, thoughts and ego will no*thing* be left to be realized. Thus we cannot realize Brahman with anything; in fact all things including our thoughts are a hindrance to realizing Brahman.

If you have any questions, doubts, suggestions or would simply like to get in touch feel free to email your query to the following email address:

**SukhdevOnline@gmail.com**

Vedanta Examples Simplified

# ABOUT THE AUTHOR

Sukhdev Virdee was born and brought up in Nairobi, Kenya. Since childhood he was very inclined towards spirituality and music. After his studies he chose to take up music as a profession. He learnt how to play the keyboards and started performing live on stage at the age of nineteen. He later went to London and completed a BTEC in Music Production and Performance.

He later flew to Mumbai, India to pursue his dream of singing and composing music in the largest Indian Entertainment Industry. His debut pop-album became a chartbuster making him a popular household name in India and across the world. Mumbai became his home where he is known for his high energy live performances and this popularity took him to several countries across every continent on the planet to perform live for huge audiences.

A few more albums and singles followed after that. He was living the life that every young person looks up to even today. He had created a name for himself and enjoyed the name, fame and fortune that most singers dream of but never get to live. During all this he was totally oblivious of what life had in store for him in the coming years.

Just before his 40th birthday, when he was going through a rather rough patch in life, three of his friends gifted him the Bhagavad Gita out of the blue. These were friends that he met only occasionally and yet within two weeks three different people gifted him the Bhagavad Gita that would change his life completely. He read the Bhagavad Gita and felt Lord Krishna was speaking directly to him. It completely changed his outlook towards life as he followed the teachings in the Bhagavad Gita as best as he could.

Just over a year later, one fine morning after he woke up from his morning meditation and walked towards his temple in the house, his body completely froze and in an instant he had become one with the entire Universe. Time stood still and every particle of the entire Universe was alive and shining in bright golden light and he was the light. He was no longer limited to just his body or mind, he was everywhere at the same time and everything was one with him.

This Spiritual awakening experience turned his life upside down and inside out. All desires for anything worldly vanished, fear of death vanished, love and compassion for entire humanity and nature arose and he could feel and experience the Supreme Being in everything.

Not knowing exactly what had happened and what to do next, he sought out several resources before he was pointed towards the Upanishads that answered all his questions as to what had happened, what led to it and what to do after such an awakening.

After years of studying the Vedanta texts he is now an expert on non-dual Vedanta through not only intellectual and philosophical knowledge but most importantly with his own personal direct experience everyday.

He has put all his heart and soul into writing these books that include the highest knowledge of the Upanishads and his own direct experience and knowledge of the Supreme Being.

The series has been written with the absolute conviction that you, the reader, can realize your true immortal Universal Self too, that you are pure bliss and completely unaffected by all pain and suffering.

The promise of all spirituality is that one transcends pain and sorrow in this world, not that pain and sorrow don't come, but that the realized being is untouched by it. One realizes that their true nature is immortal, that they are one with the Universe. Would a being that realizes that he or she is one with the Universe ever want to accumulate anything in this world?

No, the True Saint or Sage who is Self-Realized makes do with only the very basic necessities required to live an honest decent life. They don't look to gain wealth, become famous, build an empire or any such sort of selfish activities.

Their main focus becomes serving humanity selflessly and uplifting others to help them realize their true nature so that they too can transcend suffering and realize their Oneness with the Universe. Sukhdev aims to do just that through his music, art and writing in the remaining days that he has left in this mortal body.

"I Am Consciousness"
6 Book Series
A Journey From Seeker
To Enlightened Master
Available As
E-books & Paperbacks
On Amazon & Other Digital Stores

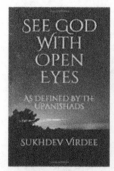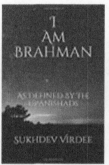

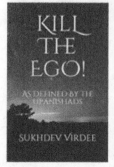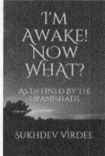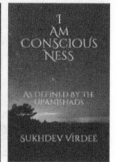

# Available As
# E-books & Paperbacks
# On Amazon & Other Digital Stores

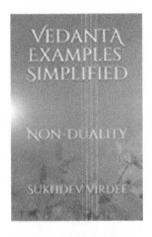

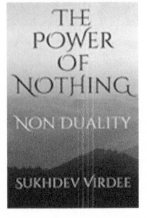
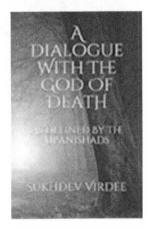

Made in the USA
Las Vegas, NV
17 October 2022

57522026R00080